Black
Preaching

HARPER'S MINISTERS PAPERBACK LIBRARY

Black Preaching

Henry H. Mitchell

Published in San Francisco by

HARPER & ROW, PUBLISHERS

New York, Hagerstown, San Francisco, London

To ELLA,
whose loving and supportive
companionship has freed
me to live and work abundantly
these thirty-five years

The author is grateful for permission to use the sermon "Jesus and Your Jailer" by the Reverend Manuel L. Scott in Chapter VIII and the sermon "The Craving for Clarity" by the Reverend Ernest T. Campbell in Chapter XI.

First Harper & Row paperback edition published in 1979.

Hardcover edition originally published by J. B. Lippincott Company in 1970.

LIBRARY OF CONGRESS CATALOG CARD NUMBER: 78-19508

INTERNATIONAL STANDARD BOOK NUMBER: 0-06-065761-8

86 87 88 89 90   10 9 8 7 6 5

Contents

Preface to the Paperback Edition

A lot of water has flowed under the bridge since the first edition of this book rushed to the press in January 1970. The ferment for the rights of the various oppressed segments of mankind has spread, taking on new aspects and opening up new fronts. The Black Revolution itself has altered its vision and strategies, and the more visible intensity has given place to a range of responses from quiet desperation to bold, imaginative involvement in the choice of a president of the United States, with two Black preachers in the highest echelons of government. Self perceptions among many Black churches have improved radically, while others resist even now the purposeful self definition and esteem of the word *Black*. Eight years of living and study have brought their changes and, I believe, improvements to my own approach to all of this, including preaching. Many more books have been written on Black religion; among them my own, on the subject of preaching:

The Recovery of Preaching (Harper & Row, 1977). The world to which this edition comes, then, is a very different world from that to which the first was addressed—different both in the Black religious sphere and in the books about it.

The question may well be asked, "Why not let *Black Preaching* rest in peace, since it has been out of print for several years?" I must confess that this question appeared plausible enough to me at first. The continuing flow of interest, however, seems to provide the answer.

There is, indeed, a clear and important difference between my more recent volume, *The Recovery of Preaching*, and *Black Preaching*. The intended target had broadened in the intervening years, but *Black Preaching*'s focus on definition and history was still apparently useful. *The Recovery of Preaching* filled the gap for which the first book was criticized, namely the methodological analysis. To this had been added a rationale for the methodology which addressed humanity as a whole. Thus there is room for both works: the first in history and definition, both for preachers and, as it turned out, for linguists and students of Black culture and history; the second for an interpretation of what the Black preaching tradition has to offer to the wider world, in the two-way street of cultural exchange which ought to prevail among Christians.

There is a second challenge which suggests the need for a revision. The Introduction, written eight years ago, admits the work to be a tentative first statement—a mere beginning in what was hoped would develop into a rich and productive dialogue about Black preaching. I hate to give the all-to-clear response to that admission: no other books have entered the dialogue, either about history or about style analysis. The bibliography at the end of this edition includes many subsequent works, but almost all of them are anthologies rather than analyses. Whatever new insights I have gained have been published in *The Recovery of Preaching* or will be forthcoming in my book on sermonic celebration. Meanwhile, as is, this first statement seems to be serving a varied and highly functional role, so I feel it wise not to interrupt the process.

Perhaps the only thing I want very much to change is the original Introduction. The attitudes I expressed and prophesied there have run their course, at least in some circles, far sooner than I predicted. When I first withdrew to observe and reflect on the Black tradition, I was quite sure that it would be generations before white churchpersons would be willing to take seriously what the Black tradition had to offer their ever less influential pulpits. As it turned out, I was wrong. Already Dr. Gardner C. Taylor and I have been asked to deliver the Beecher Lectures on Preaching at Yale Divinity School. Soon after my lectures were published as *The Recovery of Preaching*, I was launched in sharing the Black treasure in serious exchange all over America. One of the Fellows of the Martin Luther King Program in Black Church Studies has already accepted a position as associate professor of preaching and worship at Union Theological Seminary in New York City, and several seminaries of which I know have made serious offers of similar positions to Black preachers. Whatever this may or may not presage, I was overly pessimistic initially. Fortunately, it was enough to cause my withdrawal for Black reflection, without being enough to motivate a withholding of the results in lectures and publication.

Much credit for the first edition must go to Dr. C. Eric Lincoln, who supported and encouraged and offered ingenious and expert editorial suggestions. It was his initiative that kept my withdrawal from being unfruitful, while the failures are still all my own. I owe him a great debt of gratitude, and still try to follow his model of helpfulness as I assist my own students.

May the new generation of readers of *Black Preaching* find it useful, whoever they may be, serving in whatever culture.

HENRY H. MITCHELL
Claremont, California
August, 1978

Introduction

This book is born of a dream which started out along much different lines. More than twenty years ago I conceived of it as a treatise on the oneness and the fundamental unity of the verbal expressions of the Christian faith. This was based on my sincere concept of myself as a bridge-type person. I had the deep conviction of a man-in-the-middle—the belief that the differences in the faith and practice of the various racial, cultural, and theological groups were largely semantic. I honestly believed that, if I could do an in-depth study of liberals and conservatives, for instance, I could prove that they were saying the same things. I also thought that, with proper study and the passage of time, the white and Black churches with which I worked as a denominational staffer would find their way together. I am still unable to escape the deep conviction that this is the way God would have it, but I know that no book could prove it at this present stage of Christian history.

Years of frustration have crushed the hopeful idea that the proof of the unity of all varieties of American Christianity is possible in our time. The slings and arrows of outrageous half-integration, experienced at the most promising of integrationist vantage points, drove me to the solace and support of my own Black identity and of my likewise unintegrated Black Brethren. It became more and more apparent that, while it might be good to sell the great gift of Black religion to the world at large, the most important task was simply to be Black and to get myself and the Black Brethren together. Integration will come in time, but Blacks have to state what they are and what they can contribute to themselves first. Blacks must celebrate the Black contribution as it is and for themselves before they subject it to the inevitable and subtle twists of translation to another culture. This first effort, then, is toward the same goal of a raceless church; it will come. But may this harassed Black generation depart in the peace of its own understanding without having to await the far-off consummation of a church integrated through the love of Jesus Christ.

One of the most obvious and pressing reasons for a statement on Black religious culture is the need for a body of written material to be used in the burgeoning field of Black Church studies. The need for examination of the Black religious experience exists among all schools both sacred and secular, since it is crucial to Black studies; but the need to understand the Black religious experience inside the Black Church and its leadership appears to be more acute than any. An excellent example of the uniqueness of the Black religious experience is seen in the tradition of Black preaching.

Despite the widespread acceptance of Black preaching as good-according-to-white-criteria, despite the admitted strength and appeal of the best of Black preaching to Black and to white congregations, it is interesting to note that very little has been done to analyze or appropriate this strength for the sterile white pulpit. What is said in this small beginning in the field will inevitably speak to such a need, but this rich vein must first be mined for the Black people whose heritage it is, and for their children and their children's children.

Since Black preaching is by its very nature oblivious of the rules and requirements of the majority culture, the very process of reducing it to writing may cause what is said here to be in terms and forms which are not always characteristic of Black culture. But if Black preaching is to be taught rather than caught (though it must surely be both) then we shall have to adopt a communicative methodology which, foreign as it may seem, is indispensable to the job.

How does one define one's task in uncharted ground? There are many hopes and many wishes to be considered, each pressing its claim more avidly than the other. How can the young seminarians of today, for example, be encouraged to respect and extend a great tradition in creative preaching? How can they be made to understand the difference between mere imitation and being themselves a part of a tradition of personal innovation and creativity in the pulpit? How can the

virile phenomenon of Black folk-preaching undergo re-
finement, enhancing its strengths and eliminating its
weaknesses? This must be done without assault on the
integrity of Black preaching by the application of foreign criteria. As far as possible, one must speak and
evaluate from within the Black frame of reference. If
this work is found helpful by non-Blacks, then this is
only a happy coincidence. It is to the reverse coincidence of exposure to materials written for whites that
educated Black preachers owe much of what they are
today. No Black B.D. can ever fully extricate himself
from the influences, both good and bad, of three years'
systematic exposure to what goes on in the white seminary. In its own small way, this work seeks to reduce
the Black dependence on the white concept of what
preaching is all about or *should* be all about.

One of the primary goals for this work, then, is that it
be of some use to Black theological students. Whether
they are already Black-culture oriented or are becoming so, the concern is that they be assisted to communicate effectively in the Black pulpit, and most especially
to the Black masses. All too long have Black theological
graduates been so misfitted for the pulpit of the Black
Church as to be forced (where there is no benefit-of-
bishop) * to forgo the advantages of the free church
pastorate or the ministry altogether. When they have
been effective preachers in spite of their white educa-

* Black churches with no bishop tend to exercise their freedom in
favor of Black culture rather than education, where it is not possible
to call a pastor with both.

tion, they have easily escaped any negative label such as "too educated." To help the Black Brother in the Black Church, a preacher has been expected to *preach*. It is as simple as that.

One cannot, of course, be as certain of the corpus of the Black preaching tradition as he can be of the need for it. This word is offered, therefore, not as the end of the consideration but as a part of its beginning. It is offered as a first draft, a primer, a launching pad for free and frank discussion by Black students and pastors in service. It is for their stimulation in the task of developing both a better Black preacher and a better literature on Black preaching.

Severe limitations on time have necessitated that this work be brought forth for use without the long, hard criticism I would like to have given it, and without the supportive bibliography it should have. The crucial collection of tapes on which I drew—many of which are transcribed here—does not represent as careful a selection as one might have wished. But it is the best that could be gotten from very limited sources and often by the most difficult of means. Many of the most gifted of Black preachers simply do not routinely tape their messages. Others are reluctant to release them for transcription or publication. Yet this work is based on the strict assumption that Black preaching takes place only in dialogue; therefore the examples are transcripts of actual sermons as preached, with as little editing as possible. They are sermons which, in the Black tradition, were preached and *heard,* not written to be read.

Much of their real impact, therefore, is lost, unless one knows how they would have sounded and, in his mind, turns up the volume as he reads.

There is hardly a single example, then, which could not be quickly and radically improved, by careful editing and reconstruction for purposes of *reading*. Or, perhaps more accurately stated, the content of each could easily be heavied up for the intellectual expectations of a reader rather than a hearer. But before one yields to such a temptation, he must ask himself how the "improved" version would fare in Black dialogue, which is the heart of the matter. For this reason, among others, I chose to cite only actual homiletic dialogue rather than to project what a dialogue might become. Otherwise, all one can possibly do is guess. A free Black dialogue cannot be written until it has taken place, and reduced to writing, it loses the essence of what it was. Anything else must be classified as "written for reading."

In the process of preparing one of my own sermons for publication, I was struck with the possibility of many "improvements" as I listened to the tape. The idea came over and over: "If I could just preach it again!" In a few days an emergency arose in a church, and I experimented with one improvement in particular, an addition of a scriptural reference. It went over well, but it changed the whole flow of the sermon-dialogue. The result was that some of the strengths or strong points of the first version were lost altogether in the second. Yet each transcript would show what might

be thought sufficient content. In other words, a lesson
well known by an effective Black preacher was illustrated: one cannot tell it all in one sermon, no matter
how good it is. It is far more important to get people to
relate experientially to what is told than to cover the
waterfront superficially.

This kind of understanding is vital to the use of this
book. Perhaps one reason many of the finest Black
preachers avoid publication is that they have seen the
transcripts and sensed the loss of so much that is vital
when the Word that is *preached* is reduced to words to
be *read*, and they judged their own work not suitable
for publication. To offer this book for publication, even
with these caveats, requires an act of courage and an
act of faith.

This work, then, is necessarily a kind of pioneer project. It must be taken as a beginning of a discussion of
Black preaching, and not the end. If it sounds at times
entirely too enthusiastic about the Black pulpit, it must
be understood that there is no recognized need here for
the traditional critical comment on the Black preacher.
This book is concerned with the *best* of the Black
preaching tradition, the best that was inherited from
the Black Fathers. It may be that the public knows
already too much of the worst. The weaknesses I think
important are mentioned throughout the work, but
with a more concentrated critical analysis reserved for
Chapter X. In the face of all these considerations, I am
very hopeful that there will be dialogue on the issues
raised for a long time to come, and that subsequent

editions of this book, or some other book, will come much nearer to doing justice to its rich and neglected subject.

I also hope that this volume will be found helpful to preachers everywhere, but it is important to note once more that it is especially addressed to the Black preacher concerned to learn and maintain the great tradition that is his. It is, of course, possible that there may be a white preacher somewhere who is oriented to Black religious culture, just as many Blacks are white oriented. If there be such a man, more power to him. May his tribe increase! However, the typical Black professor will often have his hands full dealing with Black students who are not oriented adequately to their own culture. To help these Blacks is one of the major concerns of the book. The message of the book then is addressed to the serious Black student whose interest is preaching. It will have little relevance (except as an intellectual curio) for anybody else. So be it. Let it find its mark.

For those who think of this as a hard-line return to segregation, it should be pointed out that we are dealing with an as yet undefined phenomenon. Today, every class has to be a lab, drawing out the gifts and insights of people experienced in Black. This is comparable to LeRoi Jones' explanation of the singer James Brown's music as remaining Black, because it was performed almost exclusively for *Blacks*. Says Jones in *Blues People*, "For this reason, it could not suffer the ultimate sterility that would have resulted from total immersion in the mainstream of American culture."

Black practice preaching by Blacks in dialogue with Black congregations serves the same purpose.

For the true Black no more need be said of this all-Black class participation. For the white seminary administrator there will still be problems. One of them will be his fear that he is thereby training men for a monocultural church which will soon disappear. Then where will they be able to serve? The answers are many and hard. First of all, most B.D.-trained Black preaching has *far* more appeal in the white church already than has most white preaching, trained or untrained, in the Black church. If preaching were the only consideration, the Black churches would have to pray hard to keep their formally trained preachers from being called to more affluent white pulpits right now.

Another response would be that the church, if there still is a white one, will move so slowly toward real integration that this seminary generation and several others to come need not fear having to adjust to a white church's call. Still another is that by the time churches do integrate, their religious culture should already be so integrated as to make the multicultural Black far more attractive than a monocultural white pastor.

As to where Black preachers will be able to serve, the question need not focus exclusively on the dim future. It is a fact that many whites *today* receive seminary degrees which equip them to serve only a narrow spectrum of middle-class, north-European whites. To this pattern, or "bag," Blacks have always been exposed, and in it they will still be quite competent. The crucial question is when will the important seminaries produce white graduates who can communicate with low socio-economic classes of *whites?* The obvious fact is that Blacks, especially those who are from Black-ghetto culture, are far more prepared, in spite of education rather than because of it, to reach a wider variety of whites *and* Blacks. This is another way of saying that a white student who is privileged to sit even as an auditor to the fiery practice-preaching efforts of the Black student will be better equipped to preach to every class of whites than he would have been otherwise.

A final response to the fears of Black curriculum as "one-sided theological education" is already implied. Theological education has already been one-sided for most of its existence. We Blacks only insist that some of our side be presented. But it goes farther than this. Our culture will help balance the education of whites for whites, and, in fact, our culture may yet bring integration coming the other way down a two-way street. White Christians baptized in my own unashamedly Black-culture church make me know this possibility to be real. Then there is the blackenization of the whole jazz world, where it is both satisfying and profitable for white men to be Black. So one shouldn't be too surprised if the gospel song and the Soul sermon do to the white churches what Black culture has already done to the white world of entertainment. Black preaching or the Black hermeneutic is, after all, a valid response to the great commission we hold to *all* the world.

Black
Preaching

I

Why Hermeneutic?

It will no doubt seem strange that a book avowedly committed to Black religious culture should include a chapter on "hermeneutic." Everybody knows that's a name for a new German school of theological thought. Isn't that what everybody is trying to get away from? Or at least, isn't that what Blacks are trying to shake off? In this vein, Editor Alan Geyer of *Christian Century* writes:

Systematic theology, by and large, remains in a state of Teutonic captivity. The Aryan bias of Christian doctrine is perhaps the most serious intellectual obstacle to full ecumenical fellowship with the younger churches, to their own theological creativity and to Christian evangelism in Asia, Africa and Latin America. . . . It is not that Asian or African intellectuals in large number have forged impressive new theological systems which can redeem the West if the West will but listen to them; the tragedy is that because of the confinement of even non-

Western theologians in Teutonic captivity very few indigenous theologies have emerged. . . .[1]

Black Christianity is in a bit of the same condition as
Asian, African, and Latin American Christianity. The
difference is that the Black brand has been on its own
much longer. The faith once delivered by the white
man has had more chance to indigenize itself. The fact
that Black and white were in closer physical proximity
was unimportant. Their worlds were far removed. Segregation was king. And the Black man was master of his
own church, if master of nothing else.

Thus, Black religion does in fact have more of its
own theology. It just hasn't been committed to writing
by the Black Church. In fact, it has only recently become aware that it has anything worth preserving. Now
that this self-respect has dawned, there is still the problem of a language in which to frame it. In the absence
of something better, we seem to have no other choice
than to borrow from the existing theological jargons.
The term "hermeneutic" seems to provide the handiest
vehicle for launching an experiment in Black preaching.

In other words, the best way to be sure a learned
Black (or anyone else who is theologically literate)
knows what is being proposed is to suggest that the
Black hermeneutic is parallel to the "new hermeneutic"
of Gerhard Ebeling and others. In fact, it may be both
significant and accurate to say that the Black herme-

[1] Alan Geyer, "Toward a Convivial Theology," *The Christian Century*, Vol. LXXXVI, No. 17 (April 23, 1969), p. 542.

neutic is actually a better example of this new hermeneutic than is likely to be found generally, in the
preaching traditions of modern Europe or America in
the white churches. This is true because the Black
preacher, even when he is learned, is often less inhibited than his white colleague because of his commitment to contemporary Black language, figures and experience. However there is probably no need to seek to
legitimize the Black hermeneutic by the criteria of the
new hermeneutic school of thought. Indeed, the process may in due season be reversed. Black proclamation
may very well make the new hermeneutic more intelli-
gible and meaningful. The Black approach to proclamation, rooted in the past and matured in the present,
is far more understandable to ordinary people than the
abstruse German formulations of the new hermeneutic.
If the chief task of hermeneutics is to convey the revelation in its contemporary context, then Black hermeneutics far outstrip this school, which most Blacks
never heard of anyway.

Here is a sample of the hermeneutic concept and
task as it is explained by Ebeling:

> The word of God must be left free to assert itself in an
> unflinchingly critical manner against distortions and fixa-
> tions. But . . . theology and preaching should be free to
> make a translation into whatever language is required at
> the moment and to refuse to be satisfied with correct,
> archaizing repetition of "pure doctrine."[2]

[2] Gerhard Ebeling, *Word and Faith*, trans. by James W. Leitch
(Philadelphia: Fortress Press, 1963), pp. 9 and 11.

A thoughtful, intelligent Black layman browsed through a copy of Ebeling he found in my office. Noting some passages I had underlined, he asked: "Do you believe in all these changes this writer talks about? Is nothing fixed and permanent in the Christian faith?" As his pastor, I was unavoidably amused, despite the seriousness of the question. After all, the very version of the Christian faith which was implicitly defended by the layman was a highly Blackenized body of belief. Among the white reformers of the sixteenth century and their contemporary descendants, his faith would hardly have been thought of as "the" faith once delivered to the saints. So would it be with every other cultural group and its faith, if that faith is truly its own and expressed in terms of its culture. As Dillenberger says:

> This . . . does not mean the relativity of all truth, but it does mean that the absolute truth of God is always known to us concretely and appropriately in the forms of the world in which we live.[3]

The general lack of fruitful contact with whites and their churches has left Blacks free to do their own thing, translating the faith into the forms of the Black world, unhampered by the Teutonic captivity of white theology. The fresh style and vibrancy of the best of this translation, the living, working relevance of this

[3] John Dillenberger, "On Broadening the New Hermeneutic," *The New Hermeneutic,* James M. Robinson and John B. Cobb, Jr., eds. (New York: Harper and Row, 1964), Vol. II, p. 162.

hermeneutic approach are freighted with meaning for all seekers after truth, both Black and otherwise.

Just as the new hermeneutic of Ebeling and others has sought to recapture the vital message of Luther and the Reformation Fathers for the benefit of their sons, so must the Black hermeneutic seek to look into the message of the Black past and see what the Black Fathers [4] could be saying to Black people today.

In the absence of a substantial literature on Black theology per se upon which to draw, this study must necessarily concern itself rather narrowly with Black proclamation or the fruit of the Black pulpit. Here the Black tradition is rich, and the materials, while seldom written (and not easily translated to print), have managed to survive very much intact. There has been no major change in the best of Black preaching. This fact bears scrutiny, of course, since the pace of world change seems hardly to permit such changelessness save as an anachronism out of touch with life. For one thing, the proclamation of the Black Fathers survives because it was not in the mainstream of the changing world of white theology. The life style to which it spoke and speaks was and is sealed off from the erosive instability of white middle-class society. In that separate state there remain a number of constants which outweigh the apparent surface changes. No matter how much more comfortable physically the Black man is today than were his newly freed forebears, he is still far less comfortable than his white counterparts. In many

[4] This term will be further explained in Chapters II and III.

ways he is just as oppressed as ever, even though his oppression may have taken on some measure of sophistication. The vast majority of the citizens of the Black ghetto are no nearer to real acceptance and/or at-homeness in white society than they were one hundred years ago. They may in some ways be less so. It is undeniable that Black and white Protestants are further apart theologically. And they don't go to the same churches. In consequence, the fact that ghetto proclamation and religious practice should survive and prosper should surprise none save those who have predicted the death of all religion. For ordinary Black men to remain religious at all, however, they have had to do so in their own relevant Black ways—in the context of their own religious experience.

The proclamation of the Black Fathers survives also because, in its isolation from the mainstream, it spoke and it speaks peculiarly to the needs of Black men. Unscathed by the proud abstractions of the Western world—born in Greece and reared in northwest Europe —Black men read the scripture and retold the story out of the context of the great Black experience stamped with their own Black African culture. To a people who were not print oriented, the gospel was preached, and in the mother tongue with all its own freshness and relevance. If, as Ebeling suggests, the gospel strives for expression, how else could it escape being in some significant sense different from the gospel as it was preached in the white overculture?

This illustrates two very sound principles advanced by the school of thought called the new hermeneutic.

The Black Fathers knew and followed these rules long before the Teutons spelled out the new hermeneutic. The first is that one must declare the gospel in the language and culture of the people—the vernacular. For some this involves resistance to a temptation to be learned and "proper." To the Black Fathers this was no problem. Innocent of schooling (indeed locked out of schools!) they were so trapped within their culture as to have no choice. The best of Black preachers today still know intuitively that they have no allegiance to any cultural criteria save the idiom of the people. Deprived of the opportunity to be scholarly by the limitations of a hostile educational system, they were forced to elaborate on a Bible story with imagination which could make it meaningful to them and their hearers. Black folk still crowd churches in this secular age just to hear the gospel spoken in these same moving and relevant terms. There can be no wonder as to why the educated contemporary Black preacher is not the least tempted to leave the Black style.

The second hermeneutic principle is that the gospel must speak to the contemporary man and his needs. The Black Fathers felt no compulsion to be orthodox or accepted. They showed no inclination to follow the literalistic interpretations which whites devised to meet white needs and justify slavery. On the contrary, they looked for the answer to Black people's needs. They never condoned slavery. Their spirituals attest to the fact that they seized on the Moses narrative and sang, "Tell ol' Pharaoh to let my people go!" as a demand for their own liberation. When they sang about "stealing away," they no doubt had some notion of the prayer closet, but there is strong reason to believe that to steal away to Jesus was to escape to freedom! Similarly, to sing "I ain't got long to stay here" is not exclusively other-worldly escape. It is the code language of the gospel of self-liberation.

Indeed even that outstanding spiritual of accommodation, "Humble yourself," was a message designed to keep more people from being slaughtered like Nat Turner and his followers. It meant, "Cool it—for the time being!" a temporary capitulation to the status quo. But no matter what its tactical wisdom, its relevance and its position in the idiom cannot be questioned. It was, like all the wisest utterances of the Black Fathers, addressed to the Black man's condition, and committed to changing that condition.

As I have used it, "hermeneutic" is a code word for putting the gospel on a tell-it-like-it-is, nitty-gritty basis. Perhaps it may happen eventually that the Word will have that much Blackness added to its connotation wherever it is used. If the goal of German hermeneutics is that of detheorizing the gospel and getting to people where they are—making it flexible—the typical German intellectual patterns simply have not allowed students of German hermeneutics to practice what they preached as compared to Black preachers. On the other hand, if the Black Fathers and their sons have not been prone to theorize overmuch, their culture and their congregations have had little place for abstractions. When Black preachers have departed from the standard Black mixture of mysticism and folk wisdom and interpreted the scriptures white style, they have risked loss of interest and audience. It is far easier to be creative when the congregation will accept nothing less. If the hermeneutic style which Black preachers have been forced to develop happens to spread outside the Black ghetto, it may yet make a contribution un-dreamed of by the Black Fathers. The depersonalized condition to which Black proclamation has been di-rected is more and more the condition of all colors and cultures in this mass society. White Christianity seems to be losing the battle to reach the crucial needs of the people who have to live in the kind of world we have fashioned for ourselves. A Blacker hermeneutic style among white preachers just might help to reverse the trend. As Lerone Bennett, Jr., says:

By the grace of God and the whip of history, black people, in the main, have not completely assimilated those values that are driving Western man to social and spiritual suicide: acquisitiveness, for example, numbness of heart and machine idolatry. To the extent that these things are foreign to the black experience, to that extent the Black man is uniquely qualified to take the lead in recasting the human values of our civilization.[5]

[5] Lerone Bennett, Jr., *The Negro Mood* (Chicago: Johnson Publishing Co., 1964), p. 73.

II

What Is Black?

The first century B.C. Greek historian Diodorus Siculus is reported as having said: "The Ethiopians . . . supposed themselves to be the inventors of worship, of festivals, of sacrifices, and every religious practice." [1] In other words, they claimed to be the spiritual fathers of Egyptian civilization. This could be interpreted to mean that an established tradition that religion was fathered by Blacks is at least as old as Christianity.

This is a possibility not to be taken lightly. It augurs not only for greater self-respect among Blacks; it may suggest that it is time they resumed their ancient role of leadership in the religious practice and value systems of the world, most especially in America. Whether for so ambitious a goal or merely for their own spiritual survival, the various groups within the Black religious

[1] Bennett, *Before the Mayflower* (Chicago: Johnson Publishing Co., 1964), p. 6.

tradition must record their actual practices and beliefs. This is vital. Ultimately they must analyze and refine them for posterity.

But to say that Blacks should "resume" their religious leadership is a bit misleading. In a sense they have never ceased to make crucial contributions to the religious welfare of the world. Certainly the answer to the question "What is Black?" must eventually arrive at what is uniquely Black in worship and preaching, but it must start with what broad characteristics and influences are unique among Blacks. Dr. W. E. B. Du Bois sums this uniqueness up well when he says:

Religion in the United States was not simply brought to the Negro by missionaries. To treat it in that way is to miss the essence of the Negro action and reaction upon American religion. We must think of the Negro as transplanting to the United States a certain spiritual entity, and an unbreakable set of world-old beliefs, manners, morals, superstitions and religious observances. . . . Of fetishism there is much misapprehension. It is not mere senseless degradation. It is a philosophy of life. Among primitive Negroes there can be . . . no such divorce of religion from practical life as is common in civilized lands. Religion is life, and fetish an expression of the practical recognition of dominant forces in which the Negro lives. To him all the world is spirit.[2]

Christianity as believed and practiced by African culture Blacks in America became a much different

[2] W. E. B. Du Bois, *The Gift of Black Folk* (New York: Johnson Reprint Corp., 1924, 1968), pp. 325–26.

thing from what the whites had in mind for themselves. The intensity of Black faith and the rapid spread of Christianity among Blacks were due in part to the fact that their deeply spiritual world view had not been contaminated by white rationalism and materialistic manipulation. What was mistaken by whites for child-like, simple faith was in fact the product of a sophisticated African spiritual heritage which had already achieved profound transcendence over material things. It had probably never occurred to Africans to mold whole bodies of believers to the ends of an exploitative economic institution as did the white Americans, even though they well knew that God as they read him was opposed to slavery. Thus Black faith towers over that of the masters more because it is Black than because it is Christian in any sense that whites could have taught Christianity to the Black man.

The all-consuming, passionate abandon so characteristic of Black culture worship has no doubt been an escape from brutal reality and a survival technique. But in a more positive sense this abandon, this *freedom* has been the evidence that spirit supersedes environment—that life at the spiritual level is real and abundant no matter what. White Christianity learned from this. It did not teach it. The sainted white mystics of Europe had never influenced large numbers of white believers in America, and their great spiritual gifts had never been put to such a brutal torture-test as American slavery represented. At its best, Black religion still retains its highly spiritual orientation. It might be assumed with some reason that the less one is exposed to white culture the easier it is to retain Black spirituality.

But I for one strongly believe that a Black man can consciously resist the white drift and retain his Black faith, while at the same time appropriating the best of white learning and technology for whatever benefits such things may hold for Black people.

Du Bois suggests that the white American spirit is characterized by concern for position, self-assertion and determination to go forward at all odds. While he reads it as the natural reaction to European oppression and American natural resources and dynamism, it "hardens and hurts our souls, it contradicts our philanthropy and religion." [3] It was this typical American spirit which was so concerned with gain as to enslave people whose spirituality could still cause them to love and tenderly minister to the needs of their oppressors.

Dr. Du Bois sums up the Black contribution to religion thus:

> This then is the gift of Black Folk to the new world. Thus in singular and fine sense the slave became the master, the bond servant became free and the meek not only inherited the earth but made that heritage a thing of questing for eternal youth, of fruitful labor, of joy and music, of the free spirit and of the ministering hand, of wide and poignant sympathy with men in their struggle to live and love which is, after all, the end of being. [4]

In addition to the spiritual dimension of Black religion as it was brought across the Atlantic, there is another dimension of what is Black: Black religion's

[3] *Ibid.,* p. 339.
[4] *Ibid.,* p. 340.

response to the underlying Black experience in America, past and present. To express more fully what, for these purposes, is meant by the term "Black religion," it is necessary to set forth both the basic commonality of all Black experience and the vast variety of experiences which within this Black commonality have shaped the contemporary assortment of Black worship forms.

No matter what part of the country a Black man comes from, he is beset with indignities traceable to the single fact that he is Black. However well-to-do economically or however extensive his formal training, however correct his behavior, a Black man can never protect himself from the fact that he is not accepted as he would be if he were white and had the same achievements. It is not even possible to be white enough in complexion to be spared the arbitrary and absurd restrictions reserved for whoever is recognized as Black. As a consequence, no Black man will ever be truly free until all Blacks are free—*i.e.*, until the white man outgrows his tribalism and his prejudice. All Blackamerican experience is united in its being conditioned by the hostile, exploitative, racist environment in which that experience takes place.

Because the culture of racism has denied the Black man the possibility of realizing his own dignity as a person, all Black religion has of necessity been concerned with the affirmation and support of Black selfhood. The more brutalized and alienated the Black group involved, the more religion has had to compensate for the scars. *All* Black religion has had to serve this function. This may be challenged on the grounds that every religion supports the ego needs of its cultus, and that Black middle-class worship differs very little from white middle-class worship. To a casual observer impressed by the *pro forma* ordering of ritual and the uncomfortable self-constraint of the Black worshippers, such an allegation may appear justified. However, beneath the white cultural façade he has adopted, the middle-class Black feels his religion more intensely than his white counterpart, because his religion, like every religion, is related to his experience, real and vicarious, and his experiences and those of the white middle class do not correspond at points which are crucial to the understanding and the expression of religion. On the other hand the commitment of many middle-class Black Christians to Black liberation inspires a paraphrase of a saying of Jesus (Matthew 16:17): "White faith and flesh and blood hath not revealed this vision of Black freedom unto thee." The very will to resist the diabolical assaults of white-racist, Christian America must surely mean that every expression within the experience of Black religion justifies its own free-standing self-concept—a unique kind of support of Black personhood. This is crucial to the process of staying alive as persons, and Black preaching has been a way of conferring being, as it were, and stimulating the assertion of selfhood in Jesus Christ through the instrumentality of the Black Church.

A wide variety of experiences and the assortment of worship forms has always existed within the broader Black unity. In the earliest Blackamerican experience there was the very contrast between the free Black and the slave experience, or between the house slave and the field-hand experience. Additional variety stemmed from how long a given person or group might be separated from Black African religion and culture, and even from a specific culture. Beyond that, throughout our history there has been an effort on the part of whites, very consciously as well as unconsciously, to exploit these differences. One Black group or class has been set against another, with the result that Black churchmen have still to learn the meaning and the power of unity. And the lines of separation and variation today follow the same general socioeconomic and cultural-educational demarcations of the earliest Black church groups.

For example, there is the distinction between Black churches of the predominantly white denominational structures and those of what emerged as wholly Black denominations. The former were and are often much more militantly involved in the liberation of Blacks than their Black denominational counterparts; but their culture, including their religious culture, tends to be much closer to middle-class white than to that of the Black masses. This cultural cleavage has almost always been misread as resistance to education on the part of the Black masses. In fact, however, their hesitations about white intellectualism were in large part a silent resistance to being served in a culture foreign to their own.

In the post-Civil War history of the Black Baptists in Georgia, there developed an interesting cleavage over an issue of Black culture and Black Power, or self-determination. Two Black state conventions resulted from the conflict.[5] One was closely allied with the white American Baptists (sponsors of such important Black colleges as Morehouse and Spelman). The other was opposed to this Black-white alliance on grounds that could be called antipaternalism and the stifling weariness with being pressed for eternal gratitude. Underneath it were other grounds that might be interpreted today as the middle-class white cultural bias which developed in the Black colleges. The point, however, is the very strong likelihood that they were not in fact antieducation, as evidenced by the fact that they established a Black-controlled college at Macon. Although the survival rate of such schools has unfortunately been low, the educational concerns of Black-culture Baptists has been evidenced in the establishment of similar schools in nearly every state in the South, and the validity of their cultural point is seen in the effectiveness of their alumni. The same effectiveness of graduates can be claimed for the schools of Black Methodism.

An extreme example of the misreading of the cultural cleavage within the American Black community can be seen in a quotation from the history of the St. Thomas Protestant Episcopal Church of Philadelphia. This first Black Episcopal church was founded in 1794 and was led by the same Absalom Jones who joined with Richard Allen in the protest against white Methodist discrimination which ultimately produced the African

[5] Miles Mark Fisher, *The Master's Slave Elijah John Fisher* (Philadelphia: Judson Press, 1922), pp. 36–41.

Methodist Episcopal denomination. The quotation is part of an attempt on part of an early Black priest to explain the failure of the St. Thomas Church to reach large numbers of Blacks despite its deep commitment to Black education and the general welfare of Blacks:

> As Methodism addressed itself chiefly to the feelings and affections—which are always strongest among undisciplined minds—the great majority gave their adherence to that system. . . . This class of ministers, at the time referred to, made no pretensions of literary qualifications, and being despised and persecuted as religious enthusiasts, their sympathies naturally turned towards the lowly. . . .[6]

The Black priest quoted obviously had all white cultural models and no awareness of the values of the more emotionally oriented Black religious culture.

It is quite obvious that this very important church was able to reach only small numbers of Blacks because of their peculiar cultural orientation. Their unimpeachable and perhaps unparalleled commitment to Black needs was undercut by an unintentional denial of the cultural identity of the Black masses. Only recently have middle-class Americans of all races come to see the validity of what was then so summarily rejected as willful ignorance. A quotation from Dr. Harvey Cox is an illustration of the new awareness:

[6] George F. Bragg, *History of the Afro-American Group of the Episcopal Church* (New York: Johnson Reprint Corp., 1922, 1968), p. 76.

Consequently, Western Christian culture, though we rightly speak of it as "highly developed" in some senses, is woefully underdeveloped in others. It has produced too many pedestrian personalities whose capacity for vision and ecstasy is sadly crippled. . . . The awakened interest of white people in the black experience has enhanced our appreciation for a more festive and feeling-oriented approach to life. We call it "soul." [7]

Inasmuch as the more uniquely Black religious culture was developed among the Black masses, our interest is directed toward the understanding of the religion of the Black masses and especially toward the preaching which gave it its singular character. The religious culture of the Black masses was to be found in churches and missions of every denomination, but the best exemplification of what is unique and distinctive about it is found in the Baptist and the Methodist churches. The Church of God in Christ, a Black Holiness denomination founded in 1897, is one of a large and rapidly growing group of Pentecostal churches which in more recent years have developed from the Methodist-Baptist experience. It now claims a large membership among the Black masses. The religious expression common to these churches is more conditioned by their Black heritage than by their ties with white Pentecostalism. In the early 1930's the celebrated study by Mays and Nicholson showed that in Northern cities the number of Black churches of the Pentecostal-Holiness

[7] Harvey Cox, "In Praise of Festivity," *The Feast of Fools* (Cambridge: Harvard University Press, 1969), pp. 15–17.

tradition was second only to the Baptists, and today that tradition is solidly established as a salient aspect of the Black religious experience.

While the common stereotypes of the Black denominations tend to imply that the concern for education and welfare is largely outside the churches of the Black mass culture, it is interesting to note many prominent, educated black leaders, including Dr. Martin Luther King, Jr., Dr. Jesse Jackson, and Dr. Leon Sullivan, who are all products of this culture and have worked within it. Dr. Arthur Brazier, pastor of the Apostolic Church of God, is also a leader in community organization with a national reputation. The pastor/preacher model which these men represent is crucial to the Black Church. To be as relevant to the needs of Black people and as effective in leading them as Dr. King and these other well-known pastors have been, the Black preacher must understand and identify with the culture of the Black masses. But he must also possess a certain sophistication regarding the white culture which constantly surrounds and impinges upon the Black experience.

In summary it may be said that the contrasts which once characterized both ends of the Black religious spectrum are destined to become less and less important. As the Black Church gets itself together, the Black mainstream will progressively include within its scheme more and more Black churches, regardless of denomination. Disunity, even the polite kind, can hardly be afforded at a time when the Black community needs more than ever the enlightenment and the power base of the Black Church. Indeed, the emergent self-awareness of contemporary Blacks demands that all of the Black heritage be claimed and shared by all Blacks. We may expect, then, that at least to some extent, the Black hermeneutic of the Black masses will be practiced by faithful Black preachers in all Black churches, and the sophisticated modality of the middle-class churches of the Black elite will find some expression far from the style of the white middle class.

It is difficult to capture and to translate the specific characteristics of Black culture. Within the in-group it is easy to talk about because everyone knows what is meant. But when one who is not Black wants to know "just exactly what Black *is*," it is hard to say.

Perhaps the most significant overt indication of Black culture as it pertains to religion is the freedom of expression observed in the pulpit and the congregation of a given church. When a Black congregation resists white-style conformity and engages in free expression, it accords high importance to the feelings of the individual. Nowhere else in a hostile white world is his individuality as a Black man so reverenced. This acceptance is a vitally important aspect of the Black Church's role in affirming and supporting Black selfhood.

The most obvious and widespread manifestation of the Black freedom in religious practice is the custom of responding to the preaching with "Amen!" or other ejaculations. Simple "Amens!" are common in the white middle-class churches of the South also, but the spectrum of Black responses to good preaching is almost endless, and the ecstatic tone and spirit of them distinguish them quite sharply from the more hesitant and less fervent response characteristic of the white churches. The Black worshipper does not merely acknowledge the Word delivered by the preacher; he talks back! Sometimes the Black worshipper may shout. The day is not far past, if indeed it has passed at all, when the Black worshipper would consider a worship service a failure if there were no shouting. The early writings of some commentators on the Black Church suggest that there was always some resistance to this custom, but when a church arrives at the point where it frowns on the sincere ecstatic utterances of worshippers who have been moved by the Word and the Spirit, that church has clearly and concretely ceased to be Black in the fashion of the Black religious tradition.

This is not to make a shallow fetish of shouting or to offer it as the *sine qua non* of Black religion. The measure of Black authenticity, if there had to be a measure, would have to be not how much shouting is done, but out of what wellsprings of spiritual motivation it comes. The Black congregations can unerringly sense a put-on, and an insincere shouter is almost always chilled into silence by a disapproving congregation. A mature commitment to the full spectrum of Black culture would have to rule out the tendency of some Black churches to frown on the free emotional expression in religious worship. While some, and perhaps the majority, of "trained" Black clergymen (along with certain of their formally educated members) may be incapable of this emotional freedom, being Black demands that they must freely accept this very Black religious tradition. To ban it is to change the character of the Black religious service in such a way as to place the identity of that service in contention and doubt.

This is not to say, however, that formal training necessarily precludes the possibility of ecstatic utterance or shouting. More than one Black congregation has highly educated members—including trained social workers, teachers, and other professionals—whose cup runneth over on occasion. Indeed most self-consciously Black congregations will include professionals who, even though they themselves are inhibited by the values of the white middle class, are enthusiastic supporters of this emotional freedom for those who are not. The inhibited enjoy a vicarious participation in the freedom they covet but feel they can never return to. They cannot deny the presence of the Spirit even though they cannot bring themselves to take part in an overt expression of that presence and its power.

The argument over shouting involves more than its role as a signal of Blackness, or the implied issue of what criteria for worship—*i.e.*, Black or white—are being followed. Often there may be an unspoken but profound belief that the awareness of the presence of God can and should bring joy to the people, a spiritual ecstasy which cannot and should not be contained. There is a strong reverence for the sacredness of each person's personal experience with God. There is also the seldom articulated awareness that shouting is healing and cathartic, not only expressing joy at the presence of God, but also healthily purging guilt, sorrow, pain, and frustration. The new Black awareness has helped some thoughtful, sensitive Black people to appreciate the fact that Soul, the psychological underpinning that is indigenous to Black culture, cannot be separated from the emotional overflow of the worship experience. The Black man's personal religion and the Soul quality, which gives him his Blackness and makes his race, his culture and his destiny unique, grow from a single soil and spring from a common root. Soul is the supportive affirmation of Black personhood, of healing catharsis, of profound, ecstatic teaching about the presence of God. It is at once the inspiration and unification capable of getting Black people to stand up and get themselves together for the struggle.

A second and closely related characteristic of Black worship is ritual freedom. The church of the Black masses eschews a formal agenda. I do not intend to say that the printing of an order or service is never done. Rather, in the Black Church the rigid time restrictions and printed liturgical elements such as prayers, responses, etc., are foreign to the free expression characteristic of the worship of the Black majority. The early congregations of the Black masses could not have employed reading materials anyway, and the Black majority of today does not require any considerable amount of printed material. For generations many African Methodists have recited the Apostle's Creed from memory, and today the Creed takes its place alongside a congregational recitation of the Lord's Prayer or a responsive reading taken from the Bible. Most of these services are neither rigid nor prescribed. Religious freedom includes the freedom to stray from the printed program, when there is one, as well as to be very flexible about what particular items on the program may mean.

Underneath these overt exercises of freedom is the assumption that, no matter how thoroughly one prepares for worship (and modern Blacks do often insist on preparation), the final structuring of the agenda is in the hands of the Holy Spirit. God alone decides who shall take what part and how long the service shall take. The Black worship service has been left free to mediate the love and grace of God to a race of people despised and rejected by men. Why hurry? Let God's acceptance take its time. In a world of forced, hurried conformity, the Black Church remains an oasis where God and his children meet and talk to each other. "Freedom" is the key word describing this experience. Man is free. God is free. Nobody is under pressure.

A natural application of the principle of Black freedom is to be found in the music of Black worship. If the Holy Spirit is assumed to take over the specifics of a prayer or a sermon, why not the details of a musical rendition also? Thus Black worship frowns on the meticulous adherence to the printed melodic line. In Black or Soul singing, the soloist freely improvises as he is moved during the rendition. Interpretation is enriched and selfhood asserted and strengthened as it may be in few places in the Black world.

This is not limited to solo renditions. The Black congregation has melodic license, even when using a hymn book, to say nothing of when long-meter hymns are sung. The Black version of "Amazing Grace" is widely known among folk musicologists. It is hardly to be recognized as coming from the John Newton hymn now discarded by much of the white middle-class Protestant church. Yet it would be hard to imagine a church being really Black culture which did not sing "Amazing Grace," with all its usual Black improvisations. The acculturation inevitable in mass education has stimulated the use of hymn books and drawn succeeding generations further and further away from the long-meter hymn of the early nineteenth-century white Protestant, but it is still a significant element in Black worship. The church that literally suppresses the traditional music of the early Black Church can hardly be called Black. On the other hand, problems do arise when the old forms are used extensively, because of the inability of contemporary Black youth to relate to and be involved in their true musical heritage.

The long-meter music I have mentioned is an excellent example of an issue which must be faced before the question of what is Black is answered to our satisfaction. Black and white alike sang from hymn books, with no printed music and no musical accompaniment, in the late eighteenth and early nineteenth centuries, when the Black Baptists and Methodists got their start in America. Black and white, at that time, also shouted and said, "Amen!"—indeed, some white churches still engage in these practices. What then is the validity of the Black claim to uniqueness? The difference in the verbal response has already been mentioned. In addition to the wider variety of Black responses ("Tell it!"

"That's right!" "Uh-huh!" "So true!" et cetera) as compared with the white emphasis on "Amen!", there is also the fact that only Southern or sect-group whites now respond in this way at all. Middle-class white Protestantism has long since discarded audible response, although this group is now talking seriously about recovering something called dialogue. The answer to our question lies perhaps in the direction of historical, geographical, and class differences.

The Black religious culture we know today grows out of experience of the Black majority—the Black masses in America. While the Black and white mainstreams shared hymns and habits of worship two hundred years ago, the experience out of which they worshipped was radically different even then. On the basis of this divergent experience as people, it is only to be expected that they should be as widely divergent as the mainstreams of Black and white Protestant worship today. Where shouting and other phenomena of free Black worship find their parallels among whites today, these phenomena are not within the religious-culture mainstream of America. Rather, this behavior is Southern and rural, and mainly Pentecostal. Almost always it occurs among the poor, where the gap between Black and white experience is far narrower—the dispossessed whites who are in some ways more forgotten than the poverty-stricken Blacks. But even among poor whites the shouting, etc., differs greatly from the same manifestations when they occur in Black worship. For one thing, Black people are less inhibited than whites. Black freedom always seems to me to be far freer than white. Blacks seem to be much more really spontaneous. For one example, witness a telecast of a white healing service. For another, poor whites who are emotional tend to be very anti-intellectual, whereas in the Black mainstream, Blacks oppose learning only to the extent that it is not translated into their own culture where they can easily appropriate its values.

A more subtle difference was suggested to me by a Black-culture white Baptist who had had considerable exposure to emotional worship among both whites and Blacks. As he saw it, "Fiery utterance among white preachers tends to be *negative*. They speak of 'the Communist Party or the Council of Churches,' or 'Modern Science,' and they get *fiery mad*. On the other hand, Black preachers tend to be much more *positive*. They tend to be *fiery glad*." Such a risky generalization is worth exploring. It is certainly confirmed by my exposure to flaming utterance in the typical radio broadcasts of white worship services.

In the attempt to be completely fair, I must also take note of another peculiarity of the white Pentecostal-Holiness tradition. The shared emphasis on fiery experience among Black and white Pentecostals has, despite all the differences in their experiences generally, drawn them together in an uncommon racial integration of worship. The high percentage of Blacks alleged to be in the audiences and in the hierarchy of the organization of faith-healer A. A. Allen is no unique occurrence, nor is this only a recent phenomenon. In the 1940s I was personally familiar with completely mixed congregations of the Pentecostal-Holiness tradition in the states of Washington and California. Their emotionalism seemed so completely to burn away racial awareness that they publicly engaged in sincere and holy embrace, and they seemed hardly concerned whether their pastors or bishops were Black or white. A San Francisco bishop of one mixed group was a native Hawaiian. This contravention of racial customs may be less of a surprise when one considers the marginal relation certain poor whites have to the mainstream white community. The shared socioeconomic status of the Blacks and whites involved and their shared beliefs about God and worship eclipsed their concern for social convention. An important factor in this relation is the literal interpretation of the Bible, whose injunctions for love and brotherhood these sects take quite seriously. In this setting, theological Fundamentalism bears fruit in a field where many who are supposedly much more enlightened have failed completely. If this racial breakthrough were more widely characteristic of the Pentecostal-Holiness group, the latter would command a contemporary credibility worth pondering in every branch of the Christian church.

But generally speaking, in a host of ways both obvious and very subtle, the mainstream of Black worship differs as greatly from other styles of worship as do the life styles involved in each. Superficial and historical similarities are misleading, and the religious-cultural overlap between Black and white is greatly overestimated. It is as naïve to suggest that one Bible implies one religious culture as it is to suggest that one English dictionary implies one dialect and one culture throughout the English-speaking world.

To deal adequately with our central concern with Black preaching, we must devote a final consideration of the question "What is Black?" to the identity of the Black Fathers of Black preaching mentioned earlier. It is on their tradition that the Black hermeneutic of today is based, and without their contribution the term "hermeneutic," in the sense suggested by Ebeling and in use in this treatise, would have no meaning. These Black Fathers created a tradition. Its earliest development and transmission occurred without organized schools or the assistance of printed media. It was initially an oral tradition. Who, then, were the Fathers of the Black-culture preaching tradition, and who are their faithful descendants?

The term "Black Fathers" is used here to refer to Black pastors serving in Black churches which were primarily under Black control, from the late eighteenth century to the early twentieth century. This spans the period from the earliest beginnings of Black churches through the golden era of the Reconstruction Period, on down to the period of greatly increased racial repression at the turn of the century. It covers the early Black church congregations in the North and the informal gatherings of slaves for worship under the makeshift shelters called brush arbors in the South.

The term "Black Fathers" includes early freeborn preachers, slave preachers, and those who, like Richard Allen, were able to purchase their freedom. It includes,

in the earlier years, men most of whom had no formal
training whatever, for the ministry or for any other
profession, but who made strenuous efforts to establish
schools and train the men coming on behind them. It
also includes the first generation of men with some
formal training for the ministry, whether at academy,
college or seminary level, so long as they continued the
unique faith and culture delivered to the Black masses
out of which their ministerial forefathers came. In other
words, as the fathers of the religious culture of today's
Black masses, and particularly of today's Black-culture
preaching, they are defined by their freedom from—or,
where formally trained, their resistance to—the distin-
guishing errors of white religious culture.

The Black Church is a viable institution in the Black
community today because of its historic strengths and
despite its inevitable weaknesses. The Black Fathers
are defined by the extent to which they contributed to
those strengths which represent the vitality and the
viability of the church. Let us take a closer look at the
Black Fathers to see what kind of men they were.

First of all, they were interpreters of the Bible and of
religious truth, and their interpretations were designed
to meet the needs of Black people in a hostile white
world. Their concern was to comfort and strengthen
and guide their hearers, in a way not spelled out for
them by the white religious tradition but forged in the
crucible of the Black experience in America. It was
expressed in forms which were unique and characteristic of Black people and their condition. The language
and thought forms they employed were of the Black

masses, for the Black masses. The Black Fathers were powerful preachers and proclaimers. Theirs was a highly imaginative approach to the gospel, which permitted them to see the gospel's relevance to them and their people. They were especially effective in reaching the Black man's spiritual needs as well as in girding the helpless Black man to confront the perplexing array of problems which made his physical existence unpleasant and uncertain.

Most of the Black Fathers were talented organizers. The influence they won in the pulpit was used to establish church organizations, to construct church buildings and to pay off debts. They attracted mass followings and involved many in the work of the churches. At the same time they put their organizational skills to work in the Black community for the total good of the people —politically, economically, and educationally.[8]

The Black Fathers accomplished all of this against unbelievable odds and with tremendous handicaps. For instance, the First African Baptist Church of Philadelphia called the Rev. James Burrows of Northampton County, Virginia, about 1830. To free him of his obligations as a slave, two members of the church, John and Samuel Bivins, who were cousins and freemen of Philadelphia, volunteered to work in his place in Virginia until, a year later, Mr. Burrows' freedom could be purchased. Originally, the purchase money was to have been brought by him in person, but because of the Nat

---

[8] E. Franklin Frazier, *The Negro Church in America* (New York: Schocken Books, 1964), pp. 34–44.

Turner rebellion, it was determined that the money should be sent instead.[9] Imagine the concern in that congregation and the courage required by that pastor during the hysteria surrounding the rebellion! The Black Fathers, then, were men who had a native genius and a conviction that they were called by God, and they worked that call out despite their personal handicaps and the hazards incidental to the calling.

The fact that these men worked under the onus of the white man's system should not be construed to mean that they were willing to continue to do so forever. The Black Fathers labored for God, but they also worked for the political, economic and social good of God's oppressed Black children. The same Nat Turner who led the abortive rebellion aimed at freeing his people from bondage was a Baptist preacher. No description of the Black Fathers would be complete without consideration of the clear commitment many of them had to Black liberation. Some did not embrace the violence which Nat Turner saw as the only way to freedom, but many were much more dedicated to liberty than some of their descendants, and at a much greater risk. The Black Church spread early and fast because of the spiritual head start provided by African culture and the great appeal of the gospel story, but it also spread because the Blacks needed a cover under which they could assemble and plot their freedom. The notion of freedom was never far from the heart of Black

[9] Charles H. Brooks, *Official History of the First African Baptist Church, Philadelphia, Pa.* (Philadelphia: 1922), p. 22.

religion, and when one speaks of the Black Fathers and "the best of the Black Church," this active concern for Black freedom is understood. No contemporary Black preacher can be said to descend from the Black Fathers who, for whatever reason, theological or otherwise, ignores or withdraws from the struggle with which the ministry of the Black Fathers is forever identified.

In making their contribution to the Black heritage, the Black Fathers must be assumed to have started from zero in terms of white-style influence and prestige. During the early days of slavery, the Black preachers were as new to Christianity as were their hearers. They did not begin with the status of experts. This they had to earn in the face of formidable odds. They were not educated or trained. When they were permitted to preach, it was always under the ecclesiastical oversight (and quite frequently the physical oversight) of a white minister or his representative. They were not seeking power, prestige, or pecuniary profit. Indeed there was little of any of these to be had. They were after souls for Christ and liberation for man.

Richard Allen, father of the African Methodist Episcopal denomination, is a case in point. Allen finally became a pastor and ultimately a bishop but only after a series of most un-Christian maneuvers by "Christian" whites forced him to lay aside his natural humility and reluctance. Time after time, when he sought the services of white preachers for his separated group of Black Methodists, he was insulted or overcharged. The white brethren took his church away from him through legal duplicity. Not until after years of struggle, when this great man and his people were free to control their own property and their own religious destiny, did Allen accept formal leadership of his church as pastor, and finally as first bishop of the denomination.[10]

The Black Fathers, with few exceptions, had no formal education as we have noted elsewhere. When in the late nineteenth century some schooling became possible for a few men of the cloth, they quickly learned to translate their book learning into the forms and expressions which had been established by the earlier Black Fathers. Their patterns of thought, worship and proclamation were passed on in the schools they themselves founded throughout the South, and the twentieth-century Black church was blessed by numbers of Black master preachers nurtured in the tradition of the Black Fathers but polished by the Black colleges and seminaries founded by the churches.

It is important to remember again that there is a distinct Black religious experience today because there was and is a distinct Black experience in America, and because that experience was given religious interpretation by men most of whom were innocent of the white tradition. Their interpretations were made on the basis of their African background and their peculiar experience in America, as this experience could be articulated with their knowledge of the Bible. The theological

[10] *The Life Experience and Gospel Labors of the Right Rev. Richard Allen* (New York: Abingdon Press, 1960), pp. 30–35.

world has, therefore, a fresh datum of experience, far more free of the Teutonic captivity than can be found elsewhere in America.

Two men who represent the culmination of the period of the Black Fathers are Dr. Elijah John Fisher (1858–1915), pastor of the Olivet Baptist Church of Chicago, and Dr. Jacob Benjamin Boddie (1872–1936), pastor of the Bethesda Baptist Church of New Rochelle, New York.[11]

Elijah Fisher was born in La Grange, Georgia, youngest of eight boys in a family of seventeen children. Hired out to serve in a Baptist parsonage while he was still a small child slave, he received early exposure to Christian teachings and was baptized before he was six. His father was an unordained "floor preacher" in the Black congregation which met in the white church building. When Elijah John was seventeen, his father died, leaving a request that he care for farm and family. By now a free man—the late rebellion was over —when his farm chores permitted, Elijah studied. First it was for a month, under an ex-house-slave who could read. School was a dilapidated log hut. Tuition was one dollar a month. He managed to get two more months under a white missionary teacher before sale of the farm was forced by outside reverses, unrelated to his good management. He then spent two years in the mines at Anniston, Alabama, and nearly another year there as butler. Meanwhile he informally learned to

---

[11] Fisher, *op. cit.* Charles Emerson Boddie, *Giant in the Earth* (Berne, Indiana: Berne Witness Co., 1945).

read and studied grammar and arithmetic under teachers at Atlanta Baptist Seminary, later to be known as Morehouse College. At age twenty-one he was called to preach. While going to teach and preach in a small Georgia town he lost a leg in boarding the train there. After recovery he taught at La Grange and was pastor at several small country churches before being called successively to the First Baptist Church of Anniston (1883), the First Colored Baptist Church of La Grange, and (1889) the Mount Olive Baptist Church of Atlanta.

He then entered Atlanta Baptist Seminary and asked to be placed in the senior class. Fortunately, he was able to augment his already substantial reading sufficiently to pass the examinations required for the senior level. This was his only year of formal training, and it came after many years of success as a minister and teacher. A year after this he launched a two-year ministry in the Spruce Street Baptist Church of Nashville, Tennessee, and then he was called to his final ministry at the Olivet Baptist Church of Chicago (1903–15). While he never again attended formal classes, he spent many hours in his own large library and was, among other things, an intellectual giant in the Black Church.

Dr. E. J. Fisher is illustrative of the Black Fathers not only in his limited formal education and his success in overcoming tremendous handicaps, but in his charismatic church leadership and his practical involvement in Black liberation. In his brief two years at Atlanta, he studied at Atlanta Baptist Seminary, baptized twelve hundred people, was an important officer in statewide

Baptist work, greatly improved living conditions in the church community, edited a newspaper for Blacks, and personally invested in and helped to promote various small business enterprises as an example for Black people seeking economic independence. He was an outspoken defender of the rights of Black people, and he was not afraid to demand Black equality under the Constitution in his lectures delivered in the small towns of Georgia.

At Chicago Dr. Fisher repeated his successes with church building and the resolution-of-debt problems. In the twelve years of his Chicago ministry he built a church reputed to be the largest Protestant congregation in the world. He responded to demands for revival preaching from coast to coast, and launched the church in impressive programs of youth work, the stimulation of college preparation, and such humanitarian enterprises as a free-meal kitchen for the needy. He fostered performances by Black artists, and continued his support of Black economic activity by personal (and usually ill-fated) investments in such interests as a Gary, Indiana, land scheme, a mining venture, a coal-and-gas business, a print shop and a drugstore. Along with another Black Father, later A.M.E. Bishop A. J. Carey, Sr., he was very active in Republican Party politics, using his political influence for the welfare of his people. In his own clear-eyed devotion to his people, he saw some degree of militance as crucial to encouraging social change, and he was impatient with those who would leave it all to the Lord and the good white folks. In this he was no respecter of personalities, and he was known to criticize publicly Booker T. Washington on his silence on mob violence and lynching. Dr. Elijah John Fisher died at age fifty-seven, much too soon, but his record as a bearer of the Black tradition at its best will seldom be equaled.

The biography of another Black Father, Dr. Jacob Benjamin Boddie, is parallel to Dr. Fisher's at many points, but with certain interesting contrasts which offer a balancing influence on the image of the Black Fathers. The fourth of nine children born to ex-slave parents in Nashville, North Carolina, Dr. Boddie was indeed a physical giant, standing six feet seven inches tall and weighing 260 pounds, in his active adult years. He only served two churches officially, one at Scranton for six years, and the Bethesda Church at New Rochelle, where he remained twenty-nine years. A fiery and unusually energetic preacher, he was, like Dr. Fisher, in demand as a revival preacher all over America.

As a boy, Dr. Boddie gained a sixth-grade education in the rural schools near Rocky Mount, North Carolina, between crop duties. He also attended Auburn Institute at Franklin, North Carolina, for three years, and taught school for a brief period before going north. Later he ran a grocery store in Princeton, New Jersey, before moving to Philadelphia, where he worked as a hod carrier on high-building construction jobs and as an employee of an ice plant. In his efforts to get ordained he was discouraged by his Northern church connections and had to return to North Carolina. Always aware of his limitations, he worked on a coal truck to supplement his earnings even after he was pastor at Scranton.

From a formal point of view, Boddie had no college or seminary training whatever, and his only degrees were honorary doctorates. Yet he, like Dr. Fisher, read constantly and soaked up information from everywhere. After his first wife died, he married the first Black woman graduate of what became East Strouds-burg Teachers College. To this and his wide reading exposure could be added his faithful attendance at conferences at Northfield, Massachusetts, for thirty-three years. Here he picked up ideas from Archibald Robertson, John R. Mott, Robert Speer, George Buttrick, Harry Emerson Fosdick and Paul Scherer, and translated those that had potential into his own fiery Black idiom. His vivid imagination used every important source he could muster, including the professional journals, to paint pictures that gripped and lifted his audience. No matter how much he studied, he kept to simple words and illustrations. He loved to write poetry, but he was never flowery. His direct, practical approach to life was a blessing to his church—75 percent of its membership being small-town domestic servants. Yet Dr. Boddie had great appeal as a preacher among churches accustomed to a trained clergy as well as those with less sophisticated expectations.

J. B. Boddie was uniquely never out of date or out of touch with current realities. While not to be characterized as a militant, he was quite relevantly involved in the improvement of Black educational opportunities, and once led his members in the founding of a rather successful real-estate business which went down only after the typical foreclosures of the Depression. He was also very missionary minded and deeply involved in such projects as a home for the aged, in which he put considerable personal funds. He was quite active in the affairs of his denomination and a widely respected leader.

Scores of the Black Fathers and prophets before and after Dr. Fisher and Dr. Boddie were just as relevant, and they contributed to the creation and elaboration of the best of a unique Black religious tradition which was peculiarly effective in addressing the needs of Black people, and remains so to this day. This tradition may be the last best hope of saving Christianity in America from the hypocrisy and intellectualism which have so nearly choked it to death.

The properly chastened concern for learning that characterized men like Dr. Boddie and Dr. Fisher might be styled as seeking helpful truth wherever it might be found, while maintaining a basic commitment to Black religion in confident communication with Black people. It is not impossible for a Black student, with proper commitment, to accomplish similar results today despite the peculiar limitations of the white-oriented seminaries. Indeed the struggles of the Black Fathers should obligate their sons in the ministry— wherever they are trained—to sort out whatever is good, whatever is viable for Black interests, whatever can be refined and translated for the cause. If religion in America is going to survive at all, it may well be that its survival depends on what Black Christians do about it.

In short, the descendants of the Black Fathers must continue the development of religion as a warm, sincere, God-oriented commitment, as it was laid down in the tradition of the Black Fathers. At the same time they must integrate into that religion the same thirst for new insights that caused the Fathers to found schools and to search for knowledge however and wherever they could find it. The contemporary Black preacher who strives for this is indeed the Black son of the Black Father who gave Black religion to America and to the world.

New patterns of physical survival—the transition from the plantation to the ghetto—may make it unlikely for a Black man touched by God to commune at the plow and leave the field with a valid call from God and a relevant message for Black men, as has happened so frequently in the past. The pressures of the urban crisis may crush the spirit or distort the Soul poetry that once seemed to burst from humble Black diamonds in the rough. But the tradition is still alive in the churches and in their pastors, and Black men committed to that tradition and open to the leadership of God may still be used like the Black Fathers for the redemption of Black men—indeed for the redemption of all society.

III

A History of
Black Preaching

The preaching tradition of the Black Fathers did not spring into existence suddenly. It was developed after a long and often quite disconnected series of contacts between the Christian gospel variously interpreted and men caught up in the Black experience of slavery and oppression. To this experience and this gospel they brought their own culture and folkways. In ways more unique and powerful than they or we dreamed until recently, they developed a Black religious tradition. Very prominent in that Black religious tradition were Black-culture sermons and the ways Black men delivered and responded to them. The attempt is made here to piece together the way in which this essentially oral tradition began and developed. The records from which I have had to work are understandably very sketchy, and it is a pleasant surprise that even as much as is represented here could be put together from the few reprints and other documents which have become available only very recently.

Perhaps the earliest record of the conversion of Blacks in the colonies is that of "Anthony, Negro; Isabell, Negro; William, their child, baptized" on February 16, 1623, in Elizabeth City County in Virginia.[1] It is possible of course that this was a nominal rite, but concern for the Christianization of Blacks was manifest fairly soon in colonial history. In 1674, John Eliot of New England was inviting masters to send their slaves to him for religious instruction, and Cotton Mather himself started a school in Boston for the religious instruction of Blacks and Indians in 1717.[2] Meanwhile one of the earliest records of fairly large-scale instruction and conversion had been started by Anglicans in Goose Creek, South Carolina, in 1695. By 1723 a slave in St. Andrews Parish, closer to Charleston, was reported reading and writing in the study of the catechism, and from 1743 to 1763 there was a school in Charleston to train Blacks for missionary work among their fellows. It was run by two Blacks, Harry and Andrew, who had skills in reading and doctrine.[3] Numerous other instances of training and early inclusion

[1] David Henry Bradley, Sr., *A History of the A.M.E. Zion Church* (Nashville: The Parthenon Press, 1956), p. 29.

[2] Leslie H. Fishel, Jr., and Benjamin Quarles, *The Negro American: A Documentary History* (Glenview, Ill.: Scott, Foresman and Co., 1967), pp. 36–37.

[3] Carter G. Woodson, *The History of the Negro Church* (Washington, D. C.: The Associated Publishers, 1921), pp. 7–9.

of Blacks in worship and even in Communion are reported.

The earliest efforts to evangelize American Blacks were dominated by Anglican missionaries. In addition to these there was even earlier work by Catholics and Puritans. All of these were opposed by factions of their church bodies. The most united group in both the evangelization and emancipation of Blacks from the beginning were the Quakers. However, the very rapid growth of two sects in the late eighteenth century, the Methodists and the Baptists, brought a religious style and content much more suited to Black temperaments and talents. Furthermore these groups were much less prone to get stuck on technicalities related to apostolic succession or education of the clergy than were the more formal church bodies. It is easy to see how it was from their ranks that there rose up the first Black preachers of which we have any record.

It is an interesting irony that some of the very earliest Black preachers may have preached to more whites than Blacks. This may be explained by several factors. One was that, in the beginning, the number of Blacks who understood, or were permitted to hear, Christian preaching was relatively limited. Another was that many of the slave masters still held the humanity of Blacks under convenient suspicion, not being willing to raise them above the level of animal property and concede them souls in need of saving in the first place. So late and enlightened an architect of American democracy as Thomas Jefferson raised serious questions about the human qualities of Black people. Jefferson was passionately and pointedly refuted by David Walker, a Black Methodist layman of Boston.[4] On the theory that Blacks were not human, they were prohibited by some from attendance at worship or instruction. Still another factor was that, from the very beginning of slavery, the slaveholders understood very clearly what they were and how evil it was. When finally they did permit the unfortunate Blacks to hear the Word, the Word reserved for them was the pious platitudes of distorted paulinism mouthed by white preachers who suborned themselves and their calling by attempting to sell slavery to the slaves as "the will of God" rather than as the avarice of the white man. The slave-owning Christians knew full well that human bondage was incompatible with Christian love. They feared that the slaves who became their brothers in Christ might somehow arrive at the notion that to enslave your brother is scandalous! No, it would be better to keep the slaves from all contact with the church. Some truth, however inadvertent, might be discovered.[5] Preaching was not the most rewarding endeavor in colonial times, and few white men, especially in the South, were interested in it. Hence, to have a Black preacher preach to a white audience as a mere *functionary* under their control was one thing; to have one loose among the Blacks—preaching what he would—was quite another.

[4] David Walker, *An Appeal* (New York: Arno Press and The New York Times, 1829, 1969), pp. 27, 38, and 39.

[5] Woodson, *op. cit.*, pp. 17–20.

A final factor explaining the white audiences may have been that the Black preachers offered from the first not only novelty, but real talent and power. Thus some whites, in the new denominations already short of preachers, heard Blacks gladly because they had so much to offer and because they were the best preachers available.

Perhaps the best known and most widely traveled Black preacher was the Rev. Harry Hoosier, better known as Black Harry, who preached from 1784 until his death in 1810. He was the servant and companion of Bishop Asbury and reputed by some to be the greatest orator in America.[6] He preached both in the North and in the South and was capable of drawing large numbers of whites. A Southern Methodist bishop records, from Bishop Coke's journal of a preaching tour of Eastern Maryland, dated November 29, 1784, the following comment:

> I have now had the pleasure of hearing Harry preach several times. I sometimes give notice immediately after preaching, that in a little while he will preach to the blacks; but the whites always stay to hear him. . . .[7]

It is quite evident that Richard Allen, father of the African Methodist Episcopal Church, did his earliest preaching to audiences largely white. In fact, he indicates that he turned from over two years of lay preach-

[6] Du Bois, *op. cit.*, p. 332.
[7] Holland M. McTyeire, *A History of Methodism* (Nashville: Southern Methodist Publishing House, 1887), pp. 346–47.

ing and odd-jobbing among whites to try to reach his
Black brothers only after he had moved to Philadelphia
in 1786.[8]

The Rev. Lemuel Haynes fought in the Revolution
and was licensed to preach in the Congregational
Church in 1780, after which he was soon ordained.
Thereafter he held only white pastorates in Connecti-
cut, Vermont, and New York.[9] Du Bois suggests that he
received his M.A. at Middlebury College in 1804.[10] And
all his chroniclers indicate good response among those
he served.[11] Du Bois and Woodson also list numerous
other early Black preachers who preached for whites:
John Stewart, who preached also among Indians in his
Ohio ministry; Uncle Jack, a Baptist pastor in Notto-
way County, Virginia; John Chavis, a Princeton-trained
Presbyterian in Virginia and North Carolina; Josiah
Bishop of Portsmouth, Virginia, who ably led whites
willing to free him but not to call him as permanent
pastor and later served Black churches in Baltimore
and New York City; Henry Evans, who started the
white Methodist Church at Fayetteville, North Carolina, despite being ordered out of town; and Ralph
Freeman, a Baptist of Anson County, North Carolina.

The Rev. Andrew Marshall, pastor of First African
Baptist Church at Savannah from 1812 to 1856, had the

[8] Daniel A. Payne, *History of the African Methodist Episcopal
Church* (New York: Johnson Reprint Corporation, 1968, 1891) pp.
73–78.

[9] Woodson, *op. cit.,* pp. 61–65.

[10] Du Bois, *ibid.*

[11] Note: Among the records is an excerpt from his journal repro-
duced in Fishel and Quarles, *op. cit.,* pp. 70–72.

distinction, before being called to this church, of being
the missionary for the largely white Sunbury Baptist
Association of Georgia. He was able to draw large
congregations of whites as well as Blacks.[12] Marshall's
church's first pastor, George Leile, was converted at
Kiokee, Georgia, in 1773, while still a slave. Leile began
immediately to preach, both to slaves and to the
whites, at Matthew Moore's Baptist Church of which
he was a member. He was soon freed by his master to
devote his time exclusively to his preaching along the
Savannah River. He was ordained in 1775 and was
instrumental in founding or continuing the First African Baptist Church of Savannah, which may have been
meeting regularly as early as 1773. In 1778, the membership of Leile's first Black church at Silver Bluff,
Aiken, South Carolina, in the vicinity of Augusta, is
thought to have migrated or escaped to Savannah to
join the British, who promised them freedom. When
the British finally evacuated Savannah in 1782, Leile
went with them to Jamaica to protect himself from a
return to slavery, and thus became the first "foreign
missionary" from the United States.[13]

The membership figures for this church show 381
members in 1794, 800 members in 1802, 1,712 in 1818,
and 2,357 in 1829.[14] That Leile, Bryan, and Marshall
were effective and well received among Blacks seems
beyond question. But during this period, Methodists

---

[12] Edgar G. Thomas, *The First African Baptist Church of North
America* (Savannah, Ga., 1925), p. 74.
[13] *Ibid.*, pp. 14–30.
[14] *Ibid.*, pp. 39, 45, and 47.

and Baptists, North and South, had similar ingatherings. Charismatic Black preachers were to be found in many of the emerging Black churches. Before the day of great choirs and other attractions, these Black churches grew by leaps and bounds because they offered a warm fellowship in a cold, hostile world, and because there had already developed in the early churches a powerful Black preaching tradition.

As one ponders the rapid growth of the early Black Church and the other evidences of the effective leadership of the early Black preacher, two questions arise: 1.) What was their preaching like? And 2.) where did they get their preaching style or tradition?

In answer to the first question, there are recorded hints here and there, but it is only to be expected that the chief characteristics of Black style would be impossible to record in print. This would be true if one were seriously trying to record them. It is even more true when records are largely incidental. It is certainly true of records from the years preceding and following the turn of the nineteenth century. One word used often by whites in their description of Black preaching was "sonorous." There is good reason to believe that African culture influenced all Black preachers to use a musical and pleasing voice, with or without "moaning" or chanting. This aspect is taken for granted by Blacks not exposed to the preaching in other cultures for comparison, but it is interesting that many whites report being impressed by the pleasing speaking tones of Black preachers.

One person to use the word "sonorous" was the celebrated British geologist Sir Charles Lyell, who reported a visit to the First African Baptist Church at Savannah some time during Marshall's pastorate (1812–56). Since Marshall was sixty-seven years old when he was first called, Lyell's description of him as having gray hair does not rule out that the visit was relatively early in Marshall's forty-four year pastorate. Lyell's description runs thus:

> The singing was followed by prayers, not read, but delivered without notes by a negro of pure African blood, a gray-headed venerable-looking man, with a fine sonorous voice, named Marshall. He . . . concluded by addressing to them a sermon, also without notes, in good style, and for the most part in good English; so much so, as to make me doubt whether a few ungrammatical phrases in the negro idiom might not have been purposely introduced for the sake of bringing the subject home to their family thoughts . . . he compared it to an eagle teaching her newly fledged offspring to fly, by carrying it up high into the air, then dropping it, and, if she sees it falling to earth, darting with the speed of lightning to save it before it reaches the ground . . . described in animated and picturesque language, yet by no means inflated, the imagery was well calculated to keep the attention of his hearers awake. He also inculcated some good practical maxims of morality. . . . Nothing in my whole travels gave me a higher idea of the capabilities of the negroes, than the actual progress which they have made, even in a part of a slave state . . . than this Baptist meeting . . . they were listening to a

good sermon, scarcely, if at all, below the average standard of the compositions of white ministers—.[15]

The imagery Lyell refers to is also no accident. The
theme of the eagle stirring her nest is typical of Afri-
can-culture use of animal figures to teach great truths.
The Black imagination which Marshall brought to bear
on the Bible text was mature and a part of a tradition
doubtless centuries old. His skill was not a fresh mira-
cle but a result of a combination new to the English
visitor.

This much is certain: Marshall's combination of African culture and English Bible was not taught him in
any kind of formal school. The Bible was partly learned
at the feet of his predecessor and uncle, the Rev. Andrew Bryan. His use of standard English must have
been a matter of combined native skill and exposure to
standard speech and books. Schools open to Blacks
were most unusual even in the North. And most
churches were unable to pay for a Black preacher's
food, much less his training. Bishop Allen was quite
typical in his ownership of a shoe business so that he
could be independently secure. In his fifteen years as a
bishop he received only eighty dollars for his services.
In other words, early Black preachers had to make it
without schooling or support for their ministries, and
with little time for study. The skillful use of English
mentioned so prominently in early writings about Black
preachers was acquired in the face of denial of educa-

---

[15] Fishel and Quarles, *op. cit.*, pp. 135–36.

tion and without time to attend had there been a school open to them.

The vast unrecorded majority of these preachers, of whose utterances we have almost no record whatever, were still slaves or only recently free. In many cases they were not even free to preach, and certainly not to study. In reflecting on the hazards of preaching during his time as a slave, Moses Grandy of Boston tells of an uncle who must have died in North Carolina some time after the Nat Turner rebellion:

> After the insurrection . . . they were forbidden to meet even for worship. Often they are flogged if they are found singing or praying at home. . . . My wife's brother Isaac was a colored preacher. A number of slaves went privately into a wood to hold meetings; when they were found out, they were flogged, and each was forced to tell who else was there. Three were shot, two of whom were killed. . . . For preaching to them, Isaac was flogged, and his back pickled; when it was nearly well, he was flogged again and pickled, and so on for some months; then his back was suffered to get well, and he was sold. A while before this, his wife was sold away with an infant at her breast; . . . On the way with his buyers he dropped down dead; his heart was broken.[16]

Under such pressures and limitations it is only natural that there should have been some preaching that was not as saintly and sound as that recorded to have

[16] Moses Grandy, "Narrative of the Life of Moses Grandy," in *Five Slave Narratives*, William Loren Katz, ed. (New York: Arno Press and The New York Times, 1969), pp. 35–36.

been done by Pastor Marshall. Miles Mark Fisher quotes Frances Trollope's description of activities in one tent in an 1829 revival camp meeting in Indiana:

> One of these, a youth of coal-black comeliness, was preaching with the most violent gesticulations, frequently springing high from the ground, and clapping his hands over his head. Could our missionary societies have heard the trash he uttered, by way of an address to the Deity, they might perhaps have doubted whether his conversion had much enlightened his mind.[17]

However much Trollope's evaluation may have been slanted by being entrapped in English culture and unfamiliar with African culture, it is very probable that not all of the first untrained Black preachers were so grave and impressive to whites as was Marshall. There were no doubt some shallow, insincere manipulators.

There were exceptions to the general rule about the lack of schooling. Daniel Coker, who declined election as the first bishop of the African Methodist Episcopal Church, had the good fortune in his childhood to be attached to a young master who insisted on taking him to class with himself. On this foundation Coker must have built independently. He served as preacher in Baltimore, and he taught school privately. One of his former pupils was the same Rev. William Douglas,[18] rector of St. Thomas Episcopal Church in Philadelphia,

---

[17] Frances Trollope, *Domestic Manners of the Americans,* quoted in Fisher, *Negro Slave Songs in the United States* (New York: Russell & Russell, 1953, 1968), p. 33.

[18] Payne, *op. cit.,* p. 89, Vol. I.

whose comments critical of Methodist emotion [19] scarcely give due credit to the Methodist instruction which supplemented his training at the Black Episcopal school in Baltimore. Coker's "Dialogue Between a Virginian and an African Minister" is an illustration of the excellent command of the English language found in the recorded materials of some Black preachers. His flowery style was that in vogue among the whites, but it does not conceal his grasp either of the Bible or of logic, and it shows an early and eloquent devotion to Black liberation. When he has the white Virginian question the Black minister's training out of admiration for his articulateness, the minister responds that he has had no collegiate training whatever, but "God can teach me by his spirit to understand his word." [20]

This testimony that God had had to be their teacher was shared by most of the Black Fathers of preaching. The fact that they spoke and worked so fruitfully without formal training is evidence enough that God did bypass white academic structures and give America a Black religious input of unique warmth and relevance. Some who preached and taught in this tradition's first years lived and died as slaves. If and when they were allowed to teach the young, it was often an exercise relegated to slaves too old to work, who were given Bible teaching as a baby-sitting and character-building chore. The fact that there arose out of these kinds of

---

[19] Bragg, *ibid.*
[20] Daniel Coker, "A Dialogue Between a Virginian and an African Minister," in *Negro Protest Pamphlets*, Dorothy Porter, ed. (New York: Arno Press and The New York Times, 1969), p. 15.

beginnings so great a contribution is only underlined
by Bishop Payne's declaration that the first four bishops of the A.M.E. Church did not have even a com-
mon-school education.[21] In the first conferences, Richard Allen, Jr., age fifteen, took the minutes, because
there was nobody else capable of that much writing.[22]
What was true of this connection of the Black Church
was true of virtually all of the rest, and surely of the
other Methodists and Baptists. Great use was made of
the very ample oral endowments of the early Black
preachers, and with or without standard English, they
called together the Black churches.

The white Methodists who for twenty years refused
to ordain men like James Varick, first bishop of the
A.M.E. Zion connection,[23] never once declared them
incompetent or raised questions about their literary
skills. It was a matter of the Zion Blacks having refused
to submit. The issue was Black Power, not Black incom-
petence. Posterity can only guess how great some of
these men must have been to achieve so much with so
little earthly evidence of advantage.

After these very earliest years of the Black Church,
and prior to the golden era of the late Reconstruction
Period, there was what Bishop Daniel Payne referred to
as the second generation of leadership. Between 1820

[21] Payne, *op. cit.*, Vol. I, p. 419.
[22] *Ibid.*, p. 16.
[23] J. W. Hood, *One Hundred Years of the African Methodist
Episcopal Zion Church* (New York: A.M.E. Zion Book Concern,
1895), p. 166.
Bradley, *op. cit.*, pp. 94–95.

and 1880 or so, this generation of leaders established some trends which must be noted because of their influence on the currents of culture within the Black churches, and thus on the Black preaching tradition.

The fusion of the best of Black culture and the best of the literary and religious elements of white Christianity had been very natural in the earliest days of the Black Church. The independent study and growth of the outstanding early preachers was bound to achieve such a fusion because they were tutoring themselves. They started with themselves and their own culture, and simply added onto the Black base. Their early vision and concern for better professional skills among Black clergy led to a second generation of clergy who were more and more formally trained. Because formal study related more closely to books, and there were no books written on Black culture, and because the teachers themselves were often well-intentioned whites, training per se became more and more white oriented. With none to espouse it, African-rooted or Black culture became progressively the sign of the lack of education. As the Black community stratified, the polarities were education, higher income and white culture on the one hand, and ignorance, low income, and Black culture on the other. Even those who felt called to lead the Black masses and were quite successful in their idiom often looked on any concessions to Black culture as necessary evils.

Daniel A. Payne, who served the A.M.E. Church as bishop from 1852 to 1896, is a well-documented example. He was the denomination's most outstanding leader and the first president of Wilberforce University. Although he was a powerful advocate of education and a recognized scholar, he was a largely self-educated man. (His only formal training was two years at a Lutheran seminary.) In the official history of this period of the A.M.E. Church, which he authored, he tells of his choice of study over travel as a means to freedom:

> There he endeavored to persuade me to travel with him, and among the inducements which he plied to my mind was the following statement: Said he, "Daniel, do you know what makes the master and servant? Nothing but superior knowledge—nothing but one man knowing more than another. Now, if you will go with me, the knowledge you may acquire will be of more value to you than three hundred dollars."—the amount of the salary promised by him. Immediately I seized the idea. Instead of going to travel as his servant, I went and chained my mind down to the study of science and philosophy, that I might obtain that knowledge which makes the master.[24]

Bishop Payne taught successfully for six years in his own private school on the basis of this self-directed study, until the South Carolina legislature closed all schools for Blacks in 1835. Ever after he had short patience with Blacks who did not share his devotion to learning. Thus he bluntly referred to the early A.M.E. ministry in these terms: "These facts indicate the illiteracy of the itinerant ministry up to 1844." [25] In 1845

[24] Payne, *op. cit.*, Vol. I, p. 277.
[25] *Ibid.*, p. vii.

when he went to serve as pastor of the Bethel A.M.E. Church in Baltimore, he recorded: "Up to that time they were regarded by the white community as the most ignorant, most indolent and most useless body of Christians in the city." [26] His use of the word "ignorant" to describe his Brethren was free and frequent.

The issue of his reaction to Black culture is best illustrated by a quote from his report on a visit to a church near Baltimore, many years later, in 1878:

> After the sermon they formed a ring, and, with coats off sang, clapped their hands, and stamped their feet in a most ridiculous and heathenish way. I requested the pastor to go and stop their dancing. . . . They broke up their ring but would not sit down, and walked sullenly away. After the sermon in the afternoon, when I had another opportunity to speak privately to the leader of the band, he replied, "Sinners won't get converted unless there's a ring." Said I: "You might sing till you fell down dead and you would fail to convert a single sinner, because nothing but the Spirit of God and the word of God can convert sinners." He replied: "The Spirit of God works upon people in different ways. At camp meetings there must be a ring here, a ring there, a ring over yonder, or sinners will not get converted." . . . These "Bands" I have had to encounter in many places, and, as I have stated with regard to my early labors in Baltimore, I have been strongly censored because of my effort to change the mode of worship, or modify the extravagances indulged in by the people. . . . To the most

[26] *Ibid.*, p. 235.

thoughtful and intelligent I usually succeeded in making the "Band" disgusting; but by the ignorant masses, . . . it was regarded as the essence of religion. . . . Someone has even called it a "Voodoo dance." [27]

It is plain to see here that Black culture had weaknesses and corruptions as well as great strengths. In this it was only typical of all cultures and all things human. Bishop Payne and others like him had good reason to want to suppress the extremes of conjuring, utter nonsense, and manipulative emotion which abounded in Methodist and Baptist churches. Frederick Douglass himself tells of his own boyhood confrontation with Black culture of this grosser sort. He was being beaten regularly and unmercifully by a master named Covey. Against his own better judgment he accepted the advice of a Black conjurer and carried a magic root in his pocket when he returned from hiding. Because it was Sunday, Covey did not beat him the first day. On the second Douglass resisted him for hours. Covey never even tried to beat him again. Sandy, the Black-culture conjurer, maintained that the root had protected him. Douglass frankly faced the fact that he would never be able to tell whether it was the root or the resistance or both.[28] If, with all his early learning, religious instruction and big-city experience, Frederick Douglass was not able to discredit the con-

---

[27] Charles S. Smith, *The History of the A.M.E. Church*, Vol. II, pp. 126, 127.

[28] Frederick Douglass, *My Bondage and My Freedom* (New York: Arno Press and The New York Times, 1855), pp. 238–49.

jurer's root, two things must be said. One is that there must have been, as always, some good or value in even this primitive approach to the solution of painful personal or social problems. The other is that surely nobody should be impatient with the slave mentality which would not give up these ancient ways of coping with problems, however corrupted they were to become at the hands of an unsympathetic, alien culture. Very few Blacks had either the skills or the experience of the sixteen-year-old Douglass with which to find any better answers.

All too often the tragedy of Black people lay in following the white man's patterns of culture and inadvertently creating a stereotype of what was least admirable in Black culture. Forgetting or taking for granted the values of Black culture which are only now beginning to be celebrated fully, they ridiculed *all* Black folkways and held up a model of excellence which was uniformly white. They threw out the baby with the bath water. Often they were themselves the unconscious exemplifications of the Black experience, but these would-be Black Anglo-Saxons assailed Black music as "corn field ditties" and shouting in worship as "the fanaticism of ignorance." It is good to know that they did not succeed completely in suppressing Black culture even in themselves, although the major credit is probably due to their rejection by the very white folks they were trying to identify with.

W. E. B. Du Bois, unquestionably the most learned scholar to write on the survival of Black religious culture in his day, made the following comment in 1924:

The down trodden black man whose patient religious faith has kept his heart still unembittered, is fast becoming the singing voice of all America. And in his song we hear a prophecy of the dignity and worth of Negro genius.

The Negro folk-song entered the Church and became the prayer song and the sorrow song, still with its haunting melody but surrounded by the inhibitions of a cheap theology and a conventional morality. But the musical soul of a race unleashed itself violently from these bonds and in the saloons. . . .[29]

Here is shown an awareness of the limitations of Black culture and of its adaptations inside white America, but there is also a profound sensitivity to the depths of the Black man's soul. A true evaluation of the Black culture sermon would have to follow lines parallel to this statement rather than to indulge in the use of pejorative terminology. The conscious, organized efforts to preserve the best of the Black heritage are well over one hundred years late, but that heritage survived its neglect and its detractors simply because it is so relevant to the spirit of Black people and to the meaning of being Black. The misguided attacks of the emerging Black intelligentsia could not change this. They could only suggest the insecurities of the attackers and the myths by which they lived.

One way to trace the way in which college-trained men slowly leavened the Black Church (to borrow a

[29] Du Bois, *op. cit.*, pp. 284–85.

phrase from Du Bois) [30] is to survey the credentials of successive generations of leadership in the Black churches. For example, the education-conscious Bishop Payne can be counted on to give the details of the educational achievements of the first generations of A.M.E. bishops, right up to the day when, in the late Reconstruction Period, so many schools had been started that the denomination could bestow the robe of bishop on graduate after graduate of its own schools. Payne summarizes thus:

> We are now prepared to see what the second generation of workers is. . . . First, in literary qualifications, they are a degree above their progenitors. Of the thirteen Bishops which we have chronicled, the first four lived and died without having attained so much as a good primary education. Bishop William Fuller Dickerson, one of nine who presided over the deliberations of the General Conferences of 1880–84, was a graduate of the classical department of Lincoln University. Every one of the present eight has attained a fair English education. The majority of them have made some progress in the ancient and modern languages, and some acquaintance with the mental and physical sciences. . . .[31]

Careful perusal of the official history exposes Payne's oversight of the fact that Bishop J. M. Brown, who served from 1868 to 1896, was a prep-school graduate from Massachusetts, with private tutoring in Latin and

---

[30] Du Bois, *The Souls of Black Folk* (New York: Fawcett World Library, 1903, 1961), p. 84.
[31] Payne, *op. cit.,* Vol. I, p. 419.

Greek and very nearly four years at Oberlin.[32] But Payne's statement is quite true on the whole, and it is exemplary in its candor as well as in its deep concern for the caliber of leadership available to the Black Church.

The history of the training of the pastors of the frequently mentioned First African Baptist Church of Savannah gives some interesting insights into the evolution of training for Black pastors. It will be remembered that Andrew C. Marshall served this church from 1812 to 1856, having had no mention of any kind of preparation, formal or otherwise, prior to assisting his uncle. He was a brilliant success in the pulpit. His successor, from 1857 to 1877, was William J. Campbell. The official church history describes him as follows:

> Rev. Campbell was born January 1, 1812, of slave parents. Being the body servant of his master, he was blessed with the advantage of extensive travel. He was intelligent, a prodigious reader, and possessed a very retentive memory. He was a close student of men and had great executive ability.[33]

This is a good example of the emergence of leadership from the ranks of the "house niggers." One of the best ways to get an education in their day was obviously that of exposure to white culture. Some learning was inevitable when one was body servant of a white aristocrat. This advantage is even more evident in the next

[32] Smith, *op. cit.*, pp. 191–92.
[33] Thomas, *op. cit.*, p. 78.

pastor, the Rev. George Gibbons, who served the church from 1878 to 1884. Of him the history says:

> Rev. George Gibbons was born in Thorny Island, S. C., November 13, 1819. He was the property of Mrs. Telfair, through whose beneficence the Telfair Academy was endowed. She was very kind to him and reared him with great care and culture. He travelled extensively with the family, going once with them to Europe. He was baptized in 1844 by Rev. Andrew C. Marshall. In 1869 he was elected a deacon of the First Church and in 1870 was licensed to preach and served as an assistant to Rev. William J. Campbell. He was called to the Bethlehem Baptist Church about 1875, and by his humble, refined and dignified bearing, won the love and esteem of his entire flock. . . .[34]

Although it was some years after the Civil War before he was licensed to preach, Gibbons' chief education was obviously considered to be his exposure and travel with his masters. In the absence of other credentials, these were the best available.

The first pastor of the First African Baptist Church to have a college degree was Dr. E. K. Love, who served from 1885 to 1900. A graduate of what is now Morehouse College, he represents the first wave of men trained in denominational schools. Dr. Love is especially significant because he represents also the emergence of a national body among Baptists, having been the first president of National Baptists. The dearth of

[34] *Ibid.*, p. 83.

Black Baptist denominational historical material is largely attributable to this lack of a national body prior to this time. Dr. Love is also an excellent example of the kind of leadership which Black preachers gave during this period, when they combined the insights of their training with the still-strong influences of their culture and identity as Blacks. The church's history says of him:

> Dr. Love was also a successful social and political leader. For years, his influence was the greatest single political force in Savannah. He made and unmade mayors and aldermen, greatly influencing the administration of the city. He was also a prominent figure in state and national Republican Conventions. . . . He was also a vigorous writer.[35]

The social-political activism of the Black-preacher tradition was in evidence from the beginning. Richard Allen and Absalom Jones were active in relief work in an epidemic which swept Philadelphia in 1793. Included in their pamphlet defending the unselfish ministries of Blacks in this catastrophe is a brief antislavery tract by Allen.[36] He was also quite outspoken as a bishop later, particularly in his opposition to the "repatriation" of Black freemen to Africa.

Black preachers were very active in the antislavery

[35] *Ibid.*, p. 91.
[36] Absalom Jones and Richard Allen, "A Narrative of the Proceedings of the Black People, During the Late Awful Calamity in Philadelphia, in the Year, 1793," *Negro Protest Pamphlets,* Dorothy Porter, ed. (New York: Arno Press and The New York Times, 1969).

movement. The writers of four of the other five protest pamphlets which appear with those of Allen and Jones were also Black preachers, although the pamphlets do not so indicate in every case. The six pamphleteers were Allen (A.M.E.), Jones (Episcopal), Daniel Coker (A.M.E.), Nathaniel Paul (Baptist), William Hamilton (A.M.E. Zion), and Hosea Easton (Congregationalist). Another Congregationalist, the well-educated Charles B. Ray, was also an early antislavery worker, along with many others [37] whose names are lost to history.

Henry Highland Garnet (1815–82) included in his busy life several Presbyterian pastorates, the presidency of Avery College, and a brief term as minister to Liberia.[38] From the day he finished Oneida Institute in 1840, he was active in a group of militants who broke with William Lloyd Garrison and his school of abolitionists which depended on moral suasion to change the South. Garnet advocated what would certainly be called Black Power and Black self-determination today. He was active in the formation of a political party committed to political action to destroy slavery, and is perhaps best known for his 1843 "Address to the Slaves of the United States of America," from which the following quote is taken:

Your condition does not absolve you from your moral obligation. The diabolical injustice by which your liber-

[37] Woodson, *op. cit.*, pp. 167–84.
[38] Ernest J. Miller, "The Anti-Slavery Role of Henry Highland Garnet" (unpublished S.T.M. thesis, Union Theological Seminary, New York, 1969).

ties are cloven down, NEITHER GOD, NOR ANGELS, OR JUST MEN, COMMAND YOU TO SUFFER FOR A SINGLE MOMENT. THEREFORE IT IS YOUR SOLEMN AND IMPERATIVE DUTY TO USE EVERY MEANS, BOTH MORAL, INTELLECTUAL, AND PHYSICAL, THAT PROMISE SUCCESS.[39]

When the caucus of Black Presbyterian ministers today takes the strong position that Blacks must wield power and exercise self-determination, they follow a tradition of Blacks of the same denomination which began with Theodore Sedgewick Wright, Garnet's pastor when he was a boy in New York City. It includes men like Samuel Ringgold Ward, who held pastorates in western New York and was a prominent antislavery orator in Garnet's time, and such later political activists as Francis J. Grimké, pastor of the Fifteenth Street Baptist Church of Washington, D. C., from 1878 to 1937 (except for four years from 1885 to 1889, when health required a warmer climate).[40] His resistance to the segregationist tendencies of the Woodrow Wilson administration in Washington is recorded in some famous letters to the President.[41]

The tradition of the Black preacher includes many who have held high political office along with their church responsibilities. Senator Hiram Revels of Missis-

---

[39] Henry Highland Garnet, *An Address to the Slaves of The United States of America,* with Walker's *Appeal,* in a publication bearing the same titles, William Loren Katz, ed. (New York: Arno Press and The New York Times, 1969), p. 93.

[40] Charlotte L. Forten, *A Free Negro in the Slave Era* (New York: Collier Books, 1953, 1961), p. 39.

[41] Fishel and Quarles, *op. cit.,* pp. 390–91.

sippi was an A.M.E. pastor. He had held charges in Indiana, Missouri, Maryland, Kentucky, and Kansas, as well as Vicksburg and Jackson, Mississippi. He had also helped raise regiments in the Civil War. Richard H. Cain was a member of the Forty-third and Forty-fifth Congresses from South Carolina, in addition to being an A.M.E. pastor and bishop. As a member of the Ohio legislature, Bishop B. W. Arnett was instrumental in getting Ohio's infamous "Black Laws" repealed. And J. W. Hood was not only a successful pastor at Charlotte but an active politician and the assistant superintendent of the North Carolina schools before becoming an A.M.E. Zion bishop.[42]

The history of civil rights is replete with the leadership and the heroism of Black preachers. The Rev. H. H. Mitchell,[43] a graduate of Lincoln University, Pennsylvania, in the class of 1876 and president of Black Baptists in Virginia in the 1890s, is remembered as the preacher who put a gun out of every window in his church to protect a Black man and his wife from lynching. One of his predecessors at the Second Baptist Church of Columbus, Ohio, was Dr. James Poindexter, remembered not only for his great spiritual leadership, but for his distinction as the first Black city councilman in Columbus, and a school-board member back in the 1880s. Woodson has this to say of him as typical of Black defenders of the ministry in the supposedly dirty game of politics:

---

[42] Woodson, *op. cit.*, pp. 167–84 and 220–46.
[43] Grandfather of the author.

Poindexter's position in this case, like that of so many others, may be stated in his own words. Addressing an audience on the "Pulpit and Politics," he said: "Nor can a preacher more than any other citizen plead his religious work or the sacredness of that work as an exemption from duty. Going to the Bible to learn the relation of the pulpit to politics, and accepting the prophets, Christ, and the apostles, and the pulpit of their times, and their precepts and examples as the guide of the pulpit to-day, I think that their conclusion will be wherever there is a sin to be rebuked, no matter by whom committed, . . . or good to be achieved by our country or mankind, there is a place for the pulpit to make itself felt and heard. The truth is, all the help the preachers and all other good and worthy citizens can give by taking hold of politics is needed in order to keep the government out of bad hands and secure the ends for which governments are formed." [44]

The consideration of all these involvements, no matter how beneficial to the welfare of Blacks, still tells us little about the preacher as preacher. The one thing that it can say is that the preaching itself was probably the most important factor in the gathering together of the Black base of political power from which and for which these preachers worked. There was a very high correlation between great preacher impact for community change and great spiritual impact in the pulpit. The pulpit was the avenue of influence beyond the church walls through its power to draw so many to the church where the influence of the pulpit could be felt

[44] Woodson, *op. cit.*, pp. 224–25.

directly. Dr. C. T. Walker of Augusta, Georgia, provides an illustration in point. Woodson says of him:

> With the possible exception of Dr. C. A. Tindley, the
> talented Methodist minister of Philadelphia, probably
> the greatest preacher of power developed during the last
> generation has been Dr. C. T. Walker. Coming under the
> influence of Christian missionaries and of the Atlanta
> Baptist College [Morehouse], he had his beginnings de-
> termined in an atmosphere of religious education. For
> forty years, excepting five years when he had charge of
> the Mt. Olivet Baptist Church, New York City, he was
> pastor of the Tabernacle Baptist Church . . . attended
> not only by thousands of his own race, but by hundreds
> of winter tourists. . . . Among these were former Presi-
> dent Taft, John D. Rockefeller. . . . With the support of
> such a large number this church undertook to supply the
> needs of the community, developing into an institutional
> enterprise with all of the activities of a social welfare
> agency. . . . Dr. Walker was interested in all things
> promoting the uplift of the race. He was founder of the
> now spacious 135th Street Branch, Young Men's Chris-
> tian Association, New York City, and figured largely in
> the establishment of a similar branch for his people in
> Augusta. . . .[45]

Although Woodson's evaluation of Walker's unique
position as a Black preacher in the late nineteenth and
early twentieth century is shared by many knowledgea-
ble Blacks across the United States, the publication of
some of those sermons would give scant evidence of

[45] *Ibid.,* pp. 244–45.

Walker's greatness in the pulpit. Nor would a book of the sermons of C. A. Tindley, who is also mentioned in the Woodson quote above, hint at the style and impact that made him so famous. His *Book of Sermons* reprints twenty-nine sermons in 153 pages, but while his content is outlined and his spiritual depth exposed, his real poetry and impact are not.[46] Completely self-educated, Tindley was ordained in the Methodist Church in 1885, serving what is known as the Tindley Temple M.E. Church from 1902 to the time of his death more than thirty years later. He will live in print in the Black churches for many generations to come, but it will be for the hymns he wrote and not the sermons. Included among the hymns he wrote are "Leave It There" and "We'll Understand It Better By and By."

We may now turn our attention to a consideration of the basic elements of the Black preaching tradition as represented in such widely acclaimed Black Fathers as C. T. Walker and C. A. Tindley.

[46] C. A. Tindley, *Book of Sermons* (Philadelphia: Tindley, 1932).

IV

The Black Context for Preaching

Of equal significance with the uniqueness of Black preaching is the uniqueness of the context in which Black preaching takes place. The Black style, which includes the pattern of call-and-response, is very easily traceable to Black African culture. Such response requires a participating audience. Black preaching has had such an audience from the beginning. It has been shaped by interaction with that audience—hammered out in dialogue with the Black Brothers and Sisters. If the Black preaching tradition is unique, then that uniqueness depends in part upon the uniqueness of the Black congregation which talks back to the preacher as a normal part of the pattern of worship. To many whites and white-minded Negroes, the dialogue between preacher and congregation has been viewed as at best a quaint overreaction of superstitious simple folk, or an exuberant, childish expression of a beautiful, childlike faith such as could never occur in truly sophisticated Christian worship. At worst it has been judged as the monkeyshines of a religious revelry reminiscent of Whittier's "Brewing of the Soma."[1] Undoubtedly at times congregations have been manipulated by the preacher; and at other times congregations have probably voluntarily readied themselves for spiritual transport as a means of escaping the rigors of living in this kind of world. Yet few preachers of any race can deny the sense of the enhancement of their own powers of proclamation in the spiritual dialogue that takes place with the typical Black congregation. Most preachers would gladly welcome such support and stimulation every Sunday if it could be accepted by their congregations. In fact, the middle-class white pulpit's need for a spiritual transfusion of this sort can hardly be overestimated. In a dying church, such vitamins for added preaching power should be welcomed, no matter what their source. In the participatory response of their congregations Black preachers have a rare resource which needs greater understanding and appreciation. Understanding may well begin with a question: What is Black dialogue besides a cultural habit? Why does it help preachers from both inside and outside of Black culture? In what understandable ways does God manage to use this originally

[1] In this poem, from which the hymn "Dear Lord and Father of Mankind" is taken, orgiastic religious rites are described with phrases like "Sensual transports, wild as vain."

African phenomenon to his glory and the uplift of men in Black America?

My studies of tapes and my observations of live preaching show a high correlation between real dialogue and the intellectual level at which the sermon is pitched. "Real dialogue" is meant here to be distinguished from habitual "perfunctory dialogue," which may say more about the individual than about the culture. There is a difference between a spirited "Amen!" which registers the considered approval of the worshipper, and the automatic, nonthinking response which may punctuate the preacher's statement about so mundane a thing as collard greens and corn bread! The responder is simply reacting without hearing. He is taking his accustomed role in the worship without bothering to know what has been said. Sometimes such a person wants the preacher to sound impressive and therefore is rooting for him as a kind of personal cheering squad, no matter what he says.

Real dialogue, on the other hand, is fairly discernible and distinguishable. It occurs characteristically in response to the preacher's reference to something that is vital in the life experience of the respondent—something he identifies with, something which elicits his asseveration. He is able to respond because he is at home; he is interested in what the preacher is saying because he is involved, crucially involved in the issues as the preacher shapes them with scriptural reference and skillful allegory.

This is not to say that such dialogue starts where the hearers are and leaves them there after the sharing and the celebration of the Word. Quite to the contrary, the best Black dialogues I have studied were uniformly prone to start with familiar biblical and living materials which stretched the thinking and increased the insights of the hearers. The familiar is used as a model for understanding the unfamiliar. Minds and spirits are propelled into the unknown along tracks or trajectories established by association with previous experiences. At times the preachers, even as did Jesus, use parables. At other times they simply engage in interpretation which unites ancient biblical insights with modern experience to give some firm word about God's will for today. The term "hermeneutic" is most fittingly applied to the mind-stretching process. A preacher who does not have this capacity flirts with boredom and the loss of his audience. Black worshippers want to be stirred; they want to have an emotional experience. But they also want to be stretched, or helped and fed. They want the cream of the Black pulpit—the kind of preaching that is highly relevant in content and charismatic in delivery. When such content and imaginative delivery grips a congregation, the ensuing dialogue between preacher and people is the epitome of creative worship. Mass participation works to increase retention. The strength of the Black tradition at its best has the ability to combine fresh insight with impact—to feed the people and yet to shake them into a recognition that the spirit of God is always moving, always dynamic. It is never weak or apologetic.

A good example of the mind-stretching process is illustrated in an unpublished sermon preached by Dr.

Vernon Johns, former president of Lynchburg College and Seminary. The sermon was preached at a session of the Hampton Institute Ministers' Conference, and the title was "On Human Destiny." The sermon stimulated enthusiastic response through the projection of a simple life illustration:

> Now, you know, your definition of home enlarges as you travel. If a man asked me in Baltimore, "Where do you live?" I would say, "1134 McCulloh Street." If he asked me in New York, "Where do you live?" I would say, "In Baltimore." If he asked me in Canada, "Where do you live?" I would say, "The United States of America." And if he asked me in Europe, "Where do you live?" I would say, "In America." You see, your definition of home enlarges as you move out. [Great response.] And if my little grandchild heard that I was dead, and asked what happened to Granddad, I would like for my daughter to say, "That which drew from out of the boundless deep turned again home." [Tremendous response.] And, you know, as I get older, instead of thinking of Farmville as my home, I like to say, as someone has said, . . . "I like to think of God who is our home." [Great response.] [2]

It has already been noted that early nineteenth-century worship among whites and Blacks was similar. It might now be inferred that audible response or dialogue disappeared from white Protestant patterns because the preaching material soared out of the intellectual reach of the congregation. This occurred, perhaps,

[2] From an undated tape.

because Protestant seminaries had engaged in a contest of oneupmanship with the graduate divisions of the liberal arts colleges, creating scholars instead of professionals skilled in reaching people. With such standard conditioning in the theological schools the white preacher might well be expected to be intellectual in his concerns rather than deal with the day-to-day issues of ordinary men. It follows that in such a school-conditioned, rarefied atmosphere, answering back (hardly characteristic of graduate homiletics!) would soon be considered by the preaching scholar impolite and disruptive. This attitude would increase the inhibitions of the less sophisticated, adding to impossibility of response already due to the sermon's dealing with issues and concepts beyond the grasp of the people. Current experiments in the middle-class church, with dialogue taking place during and after sermon, seems clearly to support this hypothesis, in that in the planning of the talk-back great care is taken to pitch the dialogue within intellectual reach of the laity involved. It is encouraging to speculate that the white model may now be drifting away from the graduate classroom and back to the pattern once shared by Blacks and whites, a response pattern with strong African roots.

Black response and participation is built on this model. It happens to square with the best educational concepts, both in starting where people are and in keeping them directly involved in the process as God's truth unfolds.

Alongside the concept of intellectual grasp is that of felt need as an element in response and participation.

To be sure, scholarly problems are important. Ontology and epistemology must be considered by someone. But how can a man dialogue with the preacher in depth when he has not so much as heard if there is such a thing as ontology, much less been gripped by the question? Black preaching at its best has stuck to problems which people confront daily and feel real needs in meeting. Black people are always preoccupied with problems, and the Black preacher has had to give strength for the current day's journey, and guidance and vision for extended survival in a brutally oppressed and absurd existence.

One of the great graces of the Black Fathers was that they were beset with no temptation to start sermons in books in the first place. They had few books. There was little alternative to a here-and-now orientation. What a learned clergyman might have styled an address or sermon on the problem of evil would, in the hands of a Black preacher, be quite different. If he dared at all to phrase it as a question like "Does God Care?" or "Is God Just?" or "Can God Deliver?" it would obviously have to be rhetorical. What the Black audience requires for the dialogue is both gut-issue themes about survival and nourishing certainty. This is what they live by. They seem to say, "Be as learned as you like. Indeed, we want a smart preacher! But talk about something we can enter into, and give us something concrete and certain."

An example of how the theme of the care of God can be illuminated with modern knowledge, maintaining both the Black dialogue and idiom, and solid certainty, is found in these excerpts from a sermon by myself on the subject of fate:

God gets blamed for an awful lot of things that he never willed should happen. We feel we have said something that makes God look good . . . never realizing how badly we have misrepresented him when we are through. . . . Every now and then I feel I ought to tell a Brother, "This is what you are doing with these coffin nails [cigarettes]." In response, the Brother all too frequently says, "Well, you know, we're not going to die before our time." What he means is that he is going to live until God cuts him down. It never dawns on him that this is a sweeping doctrinal statement. . . . Sure, we do not have the final say on how long we shall live. But it's quite another thing to say you haven't anything to do with it, because you can speed your death. You can do all sorts of things God never intended, and not be able to get back here next Sunday. [Great response.] . . .

Recently, after a funeral, I heard several people publicly state, "God took him. He loved him more than we did." Of *course* God loved him more than we. . . . His love is perfect. . . . But what they are saying is that God sent that Brother a heart attack. . . . This appears to me to be highly unlikely and . . . repulsive. . . . God may be said to have given him a weaker heart than some at birth. He was born of parents with weaker hearts. . . . But I know some other things in this particular case. He worked around the clock. He had no rest. He was beset with . . . worry. . . . Now I'm sure that the three insurance men in this church would charge you a lot less for insurance if everybody waited until God sent for him.

. . . Our lives are all too often shortened by things we have done. [Response.] . . .

One of the texts, Gen. 1:28, says: "Subdue the earth." We are inclined to say that God is the one who controls cancer, but don't you know that even cancer is here for us to subdue! . . . If we were to put as much effort into subduing cancer as we have put into subduing the Viet Cong, don't you know we'd have a cure for cancer! [Great response.] God is blamed for something he left in our own hands. . . . He's waiting for us to give it everything we've got, and he will help us as needed. [Response.] . . .

I hate to trespass on people's feelings, but I hear people asking me, "Reverend, when were you born? What month? Oh, *that* explains it." Let me tell you, that don't explain nothin'! [Great response.] All this horoscope foolishness! God doesn't hold me responsible for my decisions and then have me born under a sign so I can't help myself. You know better than that! [Great response.] . . .

In the Black preaching enterprise, the preacher's preparation starts with close identity with his congregation. Historically, being Black, he could not escape having a part in their condition even if he wanted to. Whether he was chosen from the ranks of the membership (as often occurred) or not, there was no social distance. And this is still an essential part of the Black understanding between people and preacher. When today's Black ghetto preacher seems removed by his living standards, one can be sure that he is countering it by a process called poor mouth, and by making "Aunt

Jane" and all the rest know that he needs their help and support desperately as he struggles with his load. The Black preacher must be up to his ears in the condition of his people, and out of this comes the easy dialogue between people whose lives are intimately close together—so close together that the themes which invade the consciousness of the one also invade the other.

This intimacy leads people to feel literally that they are being addressed personally. Most Black preachers, if they have held a pastorate for any length of time, have been unjustly accused on occasion of meddling and revealing confidences, because the sermon material used was so close to home for some member. Even when hearers have been most grateful for a helpful message, they have been known to ask if a relative talked with the preacher that week and revealed what was happening. On the whole, however, the closeness has been a very positive value, interpreted in love and prone to reflect the close, warm relatedness of the true Christian community. In a sense, Black audiences find it difficult not to talk back to a person so close to them. The habit of personal response to preaching persists and has become a part of the culture generally. It influences relations between pulpit and pew even where the preacher is completely unfamiliar and not a close personal figure at all. Or perhaps better said, the feeling of closeness to the messenger carries through to all preachers among those who have habitually engaged in meaningful Black dialogue.

This leads to the clear and undeniable implication that much of Black dialogue is conditioned in some sense. This is true. In theory, a preacher could intone, "Corn bread and collard greens is mighty good eatin'," and (as said earlier) just by force of habit some deacon or sister would respond with a fervent "Amen!" It is a well-known fact that some Black preachers are very adept at the use of the right clichés and the right tone to elicit audible response. But this is not the whole story. Not by any means.

No preacher can accurately predict what his reception will be or what God will accomplish through his efforts. Preachers of every race agree that very often the sermon they thought would be weakest developed the greatest response after all. Just when they thought they had laid an egg, some dear soul came up and exclaimed how very much he or she had been helped. On the other hand Black religious experience is not without examples of pulpit boasters who call their shots as unashamedly as a pool shark, and solemnly promise to "kill the people"—*i.e.*, lay them in the aisles—only to appear ludicrous in failure. To be sure, such preachers have, like the pool shark, had enough successes to have some reason to believe they will succeed again. But only the most crass and insincere would ever make the same mistake twice. Certainly the vast majority of Black preachers assume that *God* will have to help them, both directly and through the congregation's participation in the dialogue, if an in-depth spiritual happening is to occur. Meanwhile, there is a blessed unpredictability that keeps Black preachers at least a little humble and keeps their audiences in a state of expectancy, always wondering which way the truth will unfold and which direction the winds of the spirit will blow.

This inability to put the Gospel encounter on a formula basis is applauded by all but the most desperate. The more humble pastor would prefer to feel that the dialogic response, as well as the eternal results, are not wholly in his frail hands. Indeed a substantial minority of Black preachers is even suspicious of audible response, not because they object to it as a Black tradition, but because of concern about the real fruits of religion. Dr. Vernon Johns, an early advocate of Black culture and Black Power, had the following to say to a group of Black preachers at Hampton Institute:

> I really believe that in our religion so much noise is, in actuality, a substitute for action. [Loud response, laughter.] You know, when a man is impressed with something, he feels he just ought to do something about it. So what he decides to do is holler about it. [Laughter, cheers.] Let me tell you, that's a lot cheaper than acting —a *whole* lot cheaper. [Widespread responses like "Whooee!"]

However, Dr. Johns himself has extolled the lively audience more than once. And what he says is not for the elimination of dialogue, but for disciplining it. This is a different thing from making fervent dialogue predictable.

The very concept of discipline seems foreign to Black spontaneity. Yet some limits need consideration. For example, concern is often expressed for some semblance of liturgical order. The Black middle-class mind, relatively less involved in the culture of the Black masses, is from its distance, prone to fear the chaos (a stronger word for unpredictability) resulting from the dynamics of such an in-depth encounter as is found in Black-culture worship. There is also the danger that the experience-centered worship will become an end in itself, devoid of reasonable elements of enlightenment or spiritual value.

Such concerns appear smaller on the Black agenda than perhaps they should. Many sensitive, intelligent Blacks who are deeply committed to Black identity and culture have left the Black-culture church because they did not see enough discipline and positive direction to justify the huge investment of resources consumed in the Black Church.

Another concern for discipline has to do with time. There is valid reason to ask why the worship service in Black churches should take so long. Modern Black youth are turned off by services commonly lasting two and a half to three hours. Many of them leave, and still others refuse to come to church at all. Black adults of great dedication welcome the careful limitation of the service. Yet Black tradition holds that the Holy Spirit does not follow white clocks. The Spirit must have its way, and whatever God does is right on time. It is believed that the true Presence is intellectually as well as emotionally enlightening, and that it takes *time* for the Spirit to involve a congregation which must first be emptied of private concern for mundane interests.

When all this is granted, the concern for time involves more than a white-style interest in restricting

worship to sixty minutes. Today's Blacks are not interested in wasting time either. However long or short,
they prefer not to be bored with uninteresting, irrelevant announcements and presentations. Black worship
still needs, in many places, to have better planning
before and after the main fare of the sermon. To do this
will not hamper the Spirit one iota. With punctual
beginning and some sensitive preparation, a truly Black
service need not require more than one and a half to
two hours, with all the participation one could wish. All
too often longer services reflect not the activity of God
but the laxity of men.

On the other hand two hours may still exceed the
attention span of some Christians. In their willingness
to spend two whole hours meaningfully, Black congregations still evidence two differences from those who
prefer to do with less. One opinion is that Black worship is not watched but participated in—in depth.
However much Black worship appears to the outsider
to be a spectator activity, it is in fact a gripping involvement with relatively little chance for the partici-
pants to notice passage of time. Pastors who insist on
lengthy anticlimactical ad libs are chastened by the
fact that people leave when the service loses its grip.
Another opinion is that the worshipper is considered
worthy to participate, thus adding to his reward or
satisfaction. Underneath the strictest middle-class commitment to keep faith with people, respect their calen-
dars, and let "busy folks" out on time is a subtle relega-
tion of these supposedly important people to a

do-nothing, spectator role so the bases can all be touched in a hurry.

One of the Black spirituals hints that people "keep so busy praisin' Jesus they ain't got time to die." The time spent in worship is not forced. It is *enjoyed*. It is an avenue of highly satisfying self-expression. Who needs to go home? Perhaps more importantly, on the Black agenda: What could possibly take preeminence over this duty to God which is at the same time so enjoyable to the worshipper?

A final aspect of the congregational context of Black preaching is that of its contagion. The joy of those most committed has always influenced the response and the satisfaction of the entire congregation. Black preachers have come to depend very heavily on a small cadre of souls, long in prayer and receptive to the Spirit, to set the tone of the preaching dialogue.

Here again is more than meets the eye. Conceding the possibility that some few may respond fervently just by habit or to trigger a general response for the preacher, the more serious worshippers may take on several much more positive roles. Some people cheer the athlete (or the preacher) more readily when others are already cheering; yet the readily responsive are much more than mere people primers. They themselves have already been primed by prayer. It remains a fact, however, that some who are themselves so deeply involved in this Black worship experience have little appreciation and understanding of the deeper significance and positive value of what they are doing.

One very positive role is implied by all that has been said about dialogue. It is that of the stimulator or initiator of the dialogue. Somebody has to be ready to participate when the sermon begins. If Black preaching is in fact dialogue, then it must be so from the beginning of the sermon. A dull, incommunicative start may establish a pattern or structure, a relationship between preacher and congregation which cannot subsequently be changed. There simply is no dialogue when only one person is speaking.

This suggests a second role, that of showing close rapport with the speaker. It has already been noted that Black dialogue involves a kind of intimacy of feeling. Such rapport is not achieved instantaneously by everyone. If there are some whose rapport with God through prayer has made them more open to immediate communication in depth with the preacher, then this helps others to achieve a similar rapport. It says to the hesitant and the uncertain that it is safe or acceptable to open up to the Spirit that is present through the preaching of the word.

Even if the responsive readiness of some is based on less lofty reasons than prayer, an influence on the larger group may still take place, and all of this may be to the glory of God and the improvement of the gospel happening.

There is another sense in which the opening up to the preacher is only a part of a larger opening up to God and the group as a whole. Modern therapy and sensitivity training have shown the value of self-revelation. But the risk-of-disclosure factor is not readily acceptable to many Blacks. In a hostile white world, they have had to be close-lipped and poker-faced to survive. Because they have been of necessity such great actors and self-concealers, they do not readily respond to any therapeutic formula which requires self-disclosure. And yet there must be some place where Blacks can actually open up and let out feelings safely. The Black Church has been that place.

The healing catharsis inherent in the Black worship service has enabled many generations of Blacks to keep their balance and sanity in a world where other racial groups with far fewer problems have chosen suicide. Statistically speaking, suicide was until recently a disease of the American white man. The Black may have had a balm the white man didn't know. He had a religion and a religious tradition which gave him a motive for living and the freedom to live. No matter what the externals of his existence, in his church he was safe in the context of love. God's love and the love of his people. It is a blessed Black tradition. The Black congregation is one of the most dynamic and healing experiences known to man. There may be tares with the wheat, but he who leaves the field because of a few tares may starve to death in the midst of bounteous plenty. From a preacher's point of view, the Black congregation with its contagious response is the best place in the world to preach the gospel. It may also be the best place in the world to hear and be healed.

V

The Black Bible

Any understanding of Black preaching requires an adequate understanding of the Black-culture view of the Bible, because Black preaching has been centered throughout its history in the Bible. Black congregations do not ask what a preacher thinks or what is his opinion. They want to know what God has told him through his encounter with the Word of God.

There are exceptions of course, gifted preachers who manage to achieve great impact without the discipline of a biblical text. Occasionally congregations accept a convincing topical preacher who does not cite extensive biblical authority. But the vast majority of Black preaching, and probably the best of Black preaching, is based on biblical authority and insights. It is likely to issue forth as the exposition of a text of scripture. No matter how creative or inventive a Black preacher may be, in the Black-culture church he must appear to exercise his freedom within the limits of that vast and profound reservoir of truth called the Bible.

This is not quite the same thing as saying that these Blacks are bibliolaters after the manner of Fundamentalist whites. Black dependence on scripture is not slavish or literal. A Black preacher is more likely to say, "Didn't He say it!" than to be officious about what "the word of God declares!" The Black preacher uses scripture more for the interpretation of recent experience than for predicting the future or for detailed prophecy. The literal, impersonal use of the scriptures would be foreign to his mind and spirit.

The Black preacher is more likely to think of the Bible as an inexhaustible source of good preaching material than as an inert doctrinal and ethical authority. He sees it as full of insights—warm and wise and relevant to the everyday problems of a Black man. It provides the basis for unlimited creativity in the telling of rich and interesting stories, and these narrations command rapt attention while the eternal truth is brought to bear on the Black experience and the struggle for liberation. The Bible undergirds remembrance and gives permanent reference to whatever illuminating discernment the preacher has to offer.

The Black preacher does not merely use the Bible. At his best he lets the Bible use him. His intuitively flexible approach to the Bible leads him to ask, "What is the Lord trying to tell me today in this passage of scripture?" Or, "What answer for today's need does the whole sweep of the New Testament give?" And, "How may I see it and tell it in the language my people will understand?" The Black preacher is not addicted to pat, legalistic or literalistic answers. They do not work for him.

The Black preacher avoids the dead, irrelevant formulations expressed in the language and the vision of the past. When he is caught using such a crutch, he is probably desperate for material and plagiarizing; or else he has lost some of his Blackness by studying at some white school of theology. At his natural best, the Black preacher is not so concerned with historical or "objective" truth as with what might be called religious truth. He has no intention of making of the Bible a textbook in science. For one thing, when he is preaching, he is very probably not interested in science. Rather he is interested in the Bible as a reliable index to God's will for man, and in this broader concern science finds its proper perspective as one aspect of a larger reality.

This stance seems congruent with that of the gospel writers at the time they wrote. Their intent was to record what had already been widely used in the churches, and it is particularly true of most New Testament materials that this use had been homiletical. It would probably never have crossed the mind of a Luke that the kerygma was anything but a resource for preaching, just as Black preachers use it. Luke would certainly never have thought of it as a resource for literalistic resistance to science, a book that could claim to know more about natural or physical phenomena than about God's will for man. The Black devotion to the Bible is not anti-intellectual, but it steers clear of

the current intellectualisms which take the Bible
lightly because they, too, read it too literally and view
it with resultant hostility.

Within this kind of unshakable attachment to the
Bible, Black preachers do some interesting and creative
things. An illustration typical in approach (though unusual in content) may be found in the World War II
Christmas sermon of a man who combined top-level
formal education with impressive gifts in Black utterance. His pulpit was in a Southeastern church made up
of people of all walks of life, from tycoons and Ph.D.'s
to a large number of tobacco workers. His fervent statement went something like this:

> Jesus can *really* be *my* Saviour and Lord. And he has the
> same unique qualifications for all of us. You see this
> straight hair and black skin? They don't match. And
> some of us have *white* skin and *not* so straight hair. . . .
> You see, there's some question about *all* our ancestry.
> Jesus knows how we feel. When he was born, there was
> some question about *his* ancestry. He shares with the
> lowest men and races in our society the stigma of ques-
> tionable parentage.

As he spoke, this great preacher drew no raised eye-
brows. There were no theological repercussions when
he clearly implied that Jesus' lineage may not have
been traced through Joseph (in the first chapter of
Matthew) for nothing. Without insulting the sensitivi-
ties of the least sophisticated, he informed his college
students and professors that the Lordship of Christ was
for him more real and relevant without dependence on

the biological improbability of a virgin birth. Unlike either the liberal or the conservative white stereotype, he showed his intellectual integrity to the thinkers of his flock, while at the same time making Christ more real to his least schooled laborer.

In this same vein of creative integrity, I have on several occasions faced the facts about Jonah in a Black sermon. This, too, was done without doctrinal trauma among the faithful. It went like this:

> You know, the book of Jonah is one of the most important books of the Old Testament, but not because of the whale. He doesn't *need* to be *in* it. And Nineveh never *was* that big, sixty miles around, three days' journey. The book of Jonah is about something much more important: race prejudice. It's a parable or a coded message about race hatred. It's like the parable of the Good Samaritan. It leads the hearer indirectly up to somethin' you couldn't say so directly. . . .
>
> Jonah is also the *funniest* Bible story I know. If you read the third verse of the fourth chapter, you see Jonah sittin' there in the city he had saved, mad and heart-broken and fussin' at God. He didn't even want to live any more. You know why? 'Cause God had made him preach an eight-word sermon, and he had done saved over a million "white folks." Now get this: he was heart-less mad because now these Gentiles he hated weren't goin' to hell. A cat has to be awful prejudiced and bitter to save that many people and then be suicidal sorry he might see 'em in heaven. Now, just between you and me, the writer was talking to the whole bitter, prejudiced Jewish church of his time. Ain't no wonder why he had to put it in a parable!

This interpretation was given and received with reverent humor, and the response of high-school and college youth present was one of deep relief and gratitude. They were off the hook for a three-day sojourn in the belly of a whale with no oxygen. In subsequent discussions they enlarged on the role of the Bible as a book of life and not as a textbook of scientific detail. But they often also got tickled about Jonah, and their loyalty to the Bible was strengthened.

The best of Black preaching today uses scholarly insights for more than the solution of the tensions between science and religion, or faith and reason. Black preachers often use the best of biblical scholarship to add living details that would not otherwise be evident in the text. These fresh insights combined with the Black imagination often enhance the gripping realism of a message. And it must never be assumed that such scholarly insights are sought and used only by those who are formally trained. Some of the most creative and imaginative use of details from archaeological and anthropological research is made by men with no degrees, but with great gifts from God, and with such great dedication to the task of preaching that they spend most of their time reading and meditating or otherwise preparing to preach.

One of the best illustrations I know of this imaginative use of detail came to me secondhand from a Tennessee pastor who had heard a Mississippi pastor preach about handicapped heroes. The text was taken from Judges 20:16: "Among all these people there were seven hundred chosen men left-handed; every one could sling stones at a hair-breadth, and not miss." The use of scholarly findings had to do with the history and significance of left-handedness in Jewish culture.

The Mississippi pastor discovered that the Hebrew word for "left-handed" meant literally "bound in the right hand." He probably assumed from the fact that there is no other word for left-handedness that one would *never* use his left if he could possibly still use his right. In Hebrew culture the right hand was, after all, the hand of strength, blessing, and unique capacity, as well as the hand of dignity and honor. The right hand of God was the ultimate place. Starting from this, the rest was easy for the inspired imagination of the Black pastor.

Unlimited by any awareness that at least some scholars think Benjamites had a special tradition of left-handedness and logically deducing that seven hundred men could hardly have been *born* bound in the right hand, he was on good ground to assume that they must have been wounded in previous battles or wars. They were the disabled veterans of their day. But they obviously did not accept disability checks and honorable discharges. Instead, they went into a new kind of training camp and practiced until they could use their left hands to sling a stone at a hair's width and not miss.

The fact that the Benjamites turned back forces ten times their size on two days in a row seems to stem largely from their sharpshooting. Their refusal to use their handicaps for an excuse was responsible for one tribe nearly defeating the other eleven. The preacher made it plain, in a moving way, that the question, under God, is not "How much are you handicapped?" but "How much do you want to work at overcoming and compensating for it?"

In his unforgettable climax he pictured men with mangled right hands and arms marching with high spirits to the war front, with this word to all who chanced to meet them: "If you see my Mom or my Dad, tell them I won't be home for a while. The war ain't over!" So saying he clinched the point that so long as the war is on, so long as there is need and injustice, no Black man can plead his handicap and do nothing. With dedication and concentration one can make as crucial a contribution to the struggle as did these disfigured and handicapped heroes. Preaching could hardly be more relevant or more inspiring.

The Black Church's capacity to receive, appreciate and use scholarly understandings is often overlooked. The problem is not so much how scholarly or intellectual the message as how well the idea is translated. Dr. Fred Sampson of Louisville, Kentucky, was very warmly received by hundreds of women from all over America at an annual session of the National Baptist Convention, U.S.A., Inc., when he included the following in a training lecture-sermon:

I do not have time to go into it in depth, but there are certain words you ought to have in your vocabulary . . . in your talking vocabulary. The word "canon"—c-a-n-o-n, "apochryphal" . . . "versions," "translations." As you know, in the first century people lived in what is known as the oral tradition. They did not have a *written* record,

as you and I have. You have the Old Testament canon
and the New Testament canon. They were not blessed to
go to a table and get the Bible as we have it. . . . This is
why Ezra read openly, publicly from the Holy Bible, the
. . . fragments as we call them today. There are blessings
that we have and we are unaware of our blessings. We
take too lightly things that God has given us, and others
have died for what we just throw around.

"Canon" comes from the Greek word meaning "straight
rod." The New Testament canon. There were many other
books to be tested. Canon . . . can be figuratively interpreted as a straight rule, or, as you find it in Galatians, a
rule of life . . . to measure, to document, to authenticate.
And so these books by scholars were gathered together
and studied, and they had to meet a straight rod—to
classify them, to place them . . . in a . . . system. And so
these are the books that have been set aside from the
others. They are the authoritative books; they are the
inspired word of God.

Now the Apocrypha makes up a set of books that has
been accepted, but they are questionable in their author-
ity. If you look in a *big* . . . Bible, you'll find between the
Old Testament and the New Testament the . . . rest of
Ezra, the rest of Daniel, etc., on questionable authority
. . . [Mentions the translations, versions and languages.]

Now don't worry about whether this Bible is true or
not. Canonized. The word of God. God breathed. Men
inspired. God through eternity dictating to them . . .
Truly the Word of God.

On paper this does not seem very Black culture, but
the delivery made it much more so. And the point is

that the delivery-translation made it quite accepted and appreciated.

The imaginative use of helpful insights of scholars is only a small part of a much broader use of imagination to put flesh on the often skeletal narratives of the Bible —to breathe life into both the story and the truth it teaches. In addition to the scholar's details, there is a great need for more vivid but no less valid details often not given in the Bible or anywhere else, to help the hearer to be caught up in the experience being narrated, and as a result to understand better and to be moved to change. Black preaching, at its best, is rich in the imaginative supply of these details and in their dramatic use in telling the gospel stories.

One aspect of this broader imaginative tradition is that of the simple elaboration of a single word or phrase. The following taped excerpts are random examples:

> "On this rock I will build my *church*. . . ." We have so covered the image of the church up with our own little traditions and our own little private arguments and opinions until if you talk about Jesus you sound wrong.

> Dr. Fred Sampson

> "But whom say *ye* that I am?" Jesus said, "Now look, I want to get this straight now. . . . You don't insult *any*body to call him John the Baptist, because I gave him the highest compliment that any man has ever received from me. *Any*body would like to be Jeremiah or Elias. . . . But you see what *you* are saying is that I am not *any*body."

Dr. Fred Sampson

"Teach *us* to pray." Jesus' disciples were good Jews. Every good male Jew was the household priest and head of the church in his house. And surely every Jew knows how to pray. The Psalms are *full* of prayer, and everywhere one looks in the religion of the Jews . . . one sees prayer. But, strangely, as you read in Luke the eleventh Chapter . . . you hear the disciples saying, "Lord, John taught *his* disciples to pray. And prayer is the heart of *every* faith. And we have heard *you* pray. And we've been close enough at times to know that you don't quite *pray* like we pray. And since we want to follow what *you* have to say—since you are praying differently and teaching differently—we want you to teach *us* to pray."

The Author

Paul—a little deformed wanderer with the label of Tarsus on his baggage.

Dr. Gardner C. Taylor

The man on that ship that night [Paul] was a man that had been with God—a man that stood high in the world and yet a man that had been lost from sight for two years. The dynamic gospel had been shut up for more than two years. No teeming crowds stood on their heads to hear him. He had not impressed . . . that he was turning the world upside down. He was a jailbird, so to speak.

Dr. C. C. Harper

These latter examples are obviously not only elaborations but, perhaps even more, characterizations. The

Black imagination adds appropriate dimensions and details to the biblical protagonist, whether individual or group. It is common in Black sermons to hear lengthy and gripping discussions of Bible characters. The instinctive attempt is made to speak of the biblical person as one who might have known him—one who can write of Paul, for instance, as a White House employee might write of the President once he is out of office. In other words, the sketch is intended to be intimate and thus more influential on the hearer from the speaker's having been closer up.

In a sermon from Philippians 3:13–14, on forgetting the things that are behind, I once portrayed Paul to a congregation in desperate need of forgetting many things:

I suspect that a great deal of what Paul has to say is lost to us because we are not aware of what Paul was, or *who* Paul was. Paul used to be Saul of Tarsus. He was a great scholar, a great church lawyer. He was a man of high standing and reputation, of very powerful connections. He was also a jealous defender of the faith and he was, in fact, you might say, a murderer. For it was he who had incited the crowd to lynch Stephen. Paul was all of this and he writes to the Philippian Church and says: "I want to forget all of this. I want to forget how big a man I was. I want to forget that I was a Hebrew of the Hebrews—circumcised and all the rest." He goes on to say that he was, as touching the law, blameless, but he wants to forget even this. "I want to count all of it but dung," he says, "if I may know Christ and the power of his resurrection and the fellowship of his suffering." He is saying, "I could best use what is in the past as dung, or manure or fertilizer, because the most important thing for me now is to know Christ." . . .

He might also have said on the same subject of forgetting that he would like to forget his *sin*. The Saul that was of Tarsus, the Saul that he wanted to forget, was a fiery, all-out, cocksure fighter; and he was sincere—never forget it! He was *very* sincere. Yes, he led a lynch mob, but he was *sincere*. And he says now, "I want to forget this also." In fact he might have said, "I don't dare think of the eyes of Stephen as he went down beneath the hail of stones. I dare not remember the look in his eyes; it would drive me crazy! I have to forget—have to *forget* what I did!"

A very contemporary and relevant characterization based on substantial imagination as well as the biblical facts was given by Dr. Evans Crawford, dean of the Howard University Chapel, at the 1969 session of the Progressive National Baptist Convention. It was included in a theological lecture which started at 10:00 P.M. and was eagerly received. The imaginative was so well integrated with the scholarly that people who remained in the session stayed awake and involved despite the late hour. This is a great tribute both to the lecturer (who was wise enough to take lecture-depth material and make it sound like a *sermon*) and to the Black biblical tradition. Here is a transcription of parts of the tape:

You remember Moses . . . after he had committed his act of self-defense on the Egyptian taskmaster down by the brick house. You know he went away. And he went up there and he had to try to get his mind together. This is the first point, really. The responsibility of the Black Church for a theology of renewal and of relevance is to work on the mind. It's in the Bible there about the renewing of what? . . . The renewing of your *mind!* You have to get this intellectual problem all straightened out.

Now what was his problem? Don't forget. Moses was reared in the *Big House*. He was with the establishment, Brothers. . . . But what happened out there was that something *human* got him. And when they were mistreating his Brother . . . he committed—just to use the language of the day—this act of self-defense. Now what happened to him? Here's what happened to him. Here was a man who had been reared in all the values of the Egyptian culture. But yet he doesn't know what happened to him with that sudden act of identification. It's almost like some of you feel. . . . You don't burn, you don't loot, but you have known of so much commercial stealing that even though you will not advocate it, there's something in you that says, "Something here has got to be torn up." And so this was the kind of thing that was happening to Moses, I think. . . .

Now I'm keeping aware of the fact that this has got to be a serious discussion. And I mean it quite seriously. Moses was considering the problem of the nature of God, walking. And he was trying to get it straight, that sudden act of identification. That's what happens to people when they identify. Their whole value system gets all shaken up. Now I didn't say when you "rationalize." I didn't say that. I said when you *identify*, the whole thing all changes.

Whole groups also may be characterized imaginatively. The following treatment of the church members at Jerusalem and Corinth in their attitude toward Paul is quoted from another sermon on forgetting:

He was under severe suspicion, you know. When he first started preaching, they said, "That's that same fella that used to lynch us and run us from town to town, and give us fits. And he gonna come up here talking about preaching? Man, you know that fella ain't right! He's over here to get us all fixed up, and one of these days they're gonna chop us to death." That's what they said about Paul. After a while they got wise to the fact that this just wasn't gonna be and then they started saying other things about him. Up there at Corinth they said, "He can't preach a lick." And they said, "There's a fellow named Apollos who can preach rings around him!" And this *hurt* Paul; this really did. He was very sensitive about this. They said that that Apollos could really preach! He could preach till the rafters rang, and Paul just *couldn't* preach.

Paul could have gotten mad about that. But that wasn't the worst thing they said about him. You know what they were whispering around Corinth? "Girl," they were saying, "that man is *crazy!*" That's what they said. "This man gets caught up and he is seized by fits or something—we don't know *what's* the matter with that fella!" And Paul had to write in II Corinthians 5 (because he was aware and he just couldn't be completely silent on the matter)—he had to write: "Whether we be beside ourselves"—in other words if I act wild and crazy it is to God—"or whether we be sober, it is for your cause. For the love of Christ constraineth us."

I don't know whether Paul had epilepsy or not. Some people have tried to establish on the basis of this that perhaps he *did* have epileptic seizures. Whatever he had, he sure had a bad name. And he didn't go off somewhere and lick his wounds and worry, and get mad when he knew that people thought there was something wrong with him. If he couldn't get to them to talk to them, he wrote them a letter, because he knew that, if you gonna serve people and work with people, you can't sit around and worry. You gotta get *to* them and get closely associated with them—because where two or three are gathered together, the Holy Spirit can burn some of this business out. Don't stand back! [1]

A less directly imaginative aspect of Black preaching is the choice of illustrations—modern parallels to the biblical text. In the process of making the point clear, the Black experience is lifted up and celebrated, and identity is enhanced. It is just as frustrating to the religious growth of Black people to use illustrations out of white middle-class life as it is destructive of Black children's reading skills to do all their reading in middle-class "Dick and Jane" books. The Black hermeneutic task is to interpret the gospel in terms that are readily grasped and quickly identified with.

Black translation begot Black illustration in the following transcript using Black-experience parallels to Luke 9:62:

Jesus said, "No man having put his hand to the plough —no man that has told me that he's gonna follow me— has any business now to look *back* to see what happens." If you're gonna plow a furrow, you can't plow it straight

[1] From a sermon by the author.

looking backwards. You gotta pick out a fence post up on the other end of the row and you gotta plow for that mark. Don't turn your eyes, 'cause if you turn your eyes, that'll turn you *and* the mule. Any man that's put his hand to the plow and looked back is not fit for the kingdom of heaven.[2]

Here the typical experiences of a great host of Black people with rural backgrounds not only makes them feel at home, as the gospel comes alive in terms meaningful for them, but the Black experience here accurately interprets the New Testament as perhaps few other group experiences would, save that perhaps of rural Southern whites walking the same mules down the same furrows. Jesus' world was hardly more primitive and agrarian than theirs. But, more to the point, the gospel was for the people at the bottom of the totem pole, with the result that illustrations out of their lives would automatically be nearer the experience of the group for whom the gospel was originally written. It is out of this kind of experience and reasoning that Professor Cone of Union Seminary declares that a truly accurate theology today would have to be a Black theology:

Because Black Theology has as its starting point the black condition, this does not mean that it denies the absolute revelation of God in Christ. Rather it means that Black Theology firmly believes that God's revelation in Christ can only be made supreme by affirming Christ as he is alive in black people today. Black Theology is

[2] From a sermon by the author.

Christian theology precisely because it has the black predicament as its point of departure. It calls upon black people to affirm God because he affirmed us. His affirmation of black people is made known not only in his election of oppressed Israel, but more especially in his coming to us and being rejected in Christ for us. The event of Christ tells us that the oppressed blacks are his people because, and only because, they represent who he is.[3]

Black illustrations tend to stick very close to the gut-level issues of life and death, of struggle and frustration. And Black preachers tend to illustrate passages already chosen from the Bible on the basis of the same criteria. White culture in the last third of the twentieth century is prone to be concerned with other problems, but the masses of Blacks are still forced to wonder about their very survival and their ability to hold on until they receive some relief in their situation. Thus a favorite passage in the Black Bible is interpreted with a special Black emphasis on the guarantee of God not to let the pressure (as opposed to the temptation) get too great: "But God is faithful, who will not suffer you to be tempted above that ye are able" (I Corinthians 10:13b). In a favorite Black gospel song it is rendered, "He knows just how much you can bear."

The two illustrations which follow are on this same text and theme, the first by Bishop A. G. Dunston and the second by Dr. Gardner C. Taylor:

[3] James H. Cone, "Black Theology and Violence," *The Tower, Alumni Magazine, Union Theological Seminary,* Spring, 1969, p. 6.

The Suffering Soul Asks Why?

Even though God doesn't get in a hurry to relieve us, he gets there on time. He gets there *on time*. Sometimes we don't need no particular agreement. We talk about "Lord, if I have to do this—as long as I have—I don't know *what* I'll do." Let me tell you something: He will be there. He will be there. After every storm there are some trees that are still standing. There has been nobody yet that could determine how much you can stand. *No*-body knows. Every time they come out and say that, if you get over a certain temperature or below a certain temperature-cold, you'll die, and somebody lays out there and goes below it and *lives*. You hear them say, if a person gets to a certain pressure, you'll die. And then somebody comes along and some doctor is puzzled why this man's pressure is up there and he's walking around. Nobody knows *what* a human being can stand—nobody but God.

Sitting on my porch some years ago, I suddenly became aware that there was something going on across the street—people were hurrying, scurrying. Right away I knew that there must have been sickness in the house. I saw relatives come up rushing in a taxicab, rushing up in their automobiles, jumping out and running into the house and running back out. Then I knew—I knew there must have been serious illness. And after a little while, I saw a long black automobile coming up. It got in the block. The driver looked like a man looking for a number. He drove on by the house on a summer evening, and stopped the car, and took his time getting out, and reached in and got his coat, and everybody else was rushing and here he was taking his time. I wondered who he was. I thought maybe he was the undertaker putting on his coat. But then he reached in and got his little bag. Then I knew who it was. That was the doctor. You see, everybody was running quickly but this man. You see, the doctor knew from what they told him—he knew what he was going to do. And he knew that whatever was required for this case was in the bag and in his head, and so he came on up to the house leisurely strolling—knowing that he's in time.

You know, that's the way God does it. Same as you can't hurry God—so why don't you wait, just wait. Everybody's ripping and racing and rushing. And God is taking his time. Because he knows that it isn't hurtin' nearly as bad as you and I think it's hurtin'—and that is the way he wants us to go. But by and by he brings relief. . . .

Bishop A. G. Dunston

From Our Awful Dignity

I preached in a certain church the other Sunday. There came down after the service a doctor who teaches in a medical school. And he came up to me, and tears came into my eyes because I remember where he came from. He and I were born in the same town. We were born not far from a sugar plantation, and now here he was teaching at a medical college. His father and mother, I suppose could—and I knew them—not read or write. And here he is now teaching at a medical college. He had gone to elementary schools where the terms were short. This doctor had battled his way—*all* of the way—I don't mean through college—I mean from elementary school on through. Seeing him brought back faces long faded and days long past.

Then he told me of how hard it had been for him. And how once he came home for the summer, not knowing whether he'd be able to go back to school or how he would get to the job out in the East that was promised to him. He did not have the money to get to the job. And he told me about a man, dearly loved of me, who let him have $65 so that he could get back to his job, so he could go to school. He said to me, "That man did not know that right then I was at the end of my courage, and if he had not given me that $65, I would have given up." Now that man *did not know*—but as surely as I stand here, my faith says to me that there was somebody who *did* know, somebody who *knows* when we reach the end of our patience, somebody who *knows* when our strength has all but failed, who knows when we've borne the last sorrow. He is the one who cares!

Dr. Gardner C. Taylor

Black illustrations are effective because they are down to earth and deal with the issues of Black existence.

In a sense, all that has been said about the Black Bible involves or implies storytelling. In another sense, effective storytelling occurs in all cultures, and there is some question as to whether there is a uniquely Black tradition in this art. There is significance in the fact that the late Dr. Clarence Jordan, a white preacher, was better than many Blacks in the art of Black translation and narration. For the purposes of this volume, however, the chief interest is to describe the technique. Too long have Blacks had to "catch" it from their fathers or pastors, or pick it up very informally wherever and however they could. The fact is that all too many Black preachers never managed to combine the gifts of a Black Bible raconteur with the skills and professional training of a bachelor of divinity. The result has been utter disillusionment for the student and impoverished leadership for the Black Church. It is probable that the one skill above all others which can open the door to influence and service is the skill of telling the story in the dramatic, imaginative Black idiom.

As is true with all good storytelling, the Black Bible story must first of all be a work of art in its own right. The teller must tell it as if the telling were an end in itself, even though he may intersperse asides to sustain the obvious relevance of the action in the story. At any time while the story is being told, the teller must be caught up in it as if he had seen it happen. In the best tradition of the folk storyteller of all cultures, he must play all the roles and make the story live. He must so communicate the story as to cause his audience to feel as if they, too, are at the scene of the action.

And yet the story must never be told for the sake of mere entertainment. The Black preacher, like the writer of a play, has a message. Plays and stories are processes which engage the vital emotions of an audience, making possible new understanding and a new orientation and commitment. No matter how charming the story or how captivated the audience, the Black preacher must take care of business and lead the hearer to do something about the challenge of this part of the Word of God. The response so often and so freely generated by this great art must be focused beyond the teller to the source of the message, and to his will for the worshipper.

It is not uncommon to find modern-day Black clergymen with professional learning who view this folk art with suspicion on the grounds that it gives the story-teller-preacher unwarranted power over an audience. Such concern is not without justification. But it is perhaps more dangerous, both for the church and the world, to nourish a pulpit tradition with all light and no heat, or with great truth, supposedly, and no charisma. If the imaginative and narrative powers of a John Jasper[4] are too much devoted to heaven and too little devoted to Black liberation, the answer is not to destroy the art. If the need for forceful communication persists, and someone has failed to employ the tools to proper ends, the answer is not, as it were, to melt the pistol but to aim and direct it more accurately on the target.

When John Jasper, one of the greatest Bible storytellers of them all, moved his nineteenth-century audience to ecstasy with his vivid views of heaven, he was very effective in welding them into a congregation and in giving their personal lives a much-needed moral quality. One can only wonder what might have been the result if the antebellum slave mentality, praised by his white racist biographers, had addressed itself to a direct concern for Black rights, education, and community life. It need not have dimmed his dramatic qualities or loosed his grip on his flock. The most he could

---

[4] Dr. John Jasper of Richmond, Va., was a peerless painter of gospel word pictures, whose fame is chiefly based on a sermon on the subject "De Sun Do Move."

have stood to lose would have been some part of his gallery of whites. There is no reason why the powers of a Jasper should not be combined with the Black liberation goals of Black preachers like Frederick Douglass or Henry Highland Garnet, or of an escaped-slave abolitionist orator like Bishop J. W. Loguen of the A.M.E.Z. church. Indeed, the model to be kept in mind in the consideration of the Black Bible story should be just such a combination. The goal of the gospel of Christ was ever to preach deliverance to the captives and to set at liberty them that are bruised.

Such a combination of Black charisma and relevance occurred when Dr. Jesse Jackson of S.C.L.C.'s Operation Breadbasket told that perennial Black favorite about the Hebrew children refusing to give up their faith. In constructing his story he pictured the Hebrews as having gotten good jobs in the government "downtown," but having refused to forget their people or surrender their identity. In the process the real message of the Bible was more accurately conveyed while the interest was heightened. The point made, of course, was that the few Blacks allowed inside the structures of the oppressor must not forget their poor Brethren in the ghetto or lose their identity and their faith.

The story of the left-handed Benjamites referred to previously is also a good example of charismatic storytelling with a contemporary kingdom goal. The Black Fathers rightly saw the same thing in stories of Moses and Samson, of David and Goliath, of Joseph and his brothers, of Paul's deliverance from prison, and of the cross and the resurrection. The Bible is full of models for the deliverance of the Black man. To tell the stories of deliverance for oppressed Jews without Black reconstruction is to jeopardize the relevance of the message for the oppressed Blacks.

In every Black Bible story, there must be a plot, with characters and conflict. There must be a protagonist or hero, and an antagonist or evil influence or bad guy. There must be suspense—curiosity as to the outcome of the conflict right up to the end. It may be as clear a cast and conflict as David and Goliath. It may be a wholly imaginary conflict, with Grace or Mercy as the protagonist and the law as the opponent, for example. The Bible base for the story may be as well spelled out as the battle of Jericho or the parable of the Prodigal Son, or it may be just a fleeting glimpse such as the parable of the Lost Coin which is told in two or three verses. In either type of situation the Black imagination is called upon to supply the details needed to establish a plot and a convincing eyewitness account.

I once heard an excellent Black version of the Prodigal Son done by a talented Black seminarian.[5] The speaker sharpened the modern understanding of the plot and characters for a Black ghetto congregation with such details as the following:

> There was nothing wrong with asking for his portion of the goods. This was expected, sooner or later. His father was happy to do with his estate what he had gathered it together for in the first place.
>
> And don't be *too* hard on the son for what he did with

[5] Charles Walker of Colgate Rochester Divinity School.

the money. He had no way of knowing there would be a famine. And none of us knows what he might do with that much money, because we never had to face that temptation and *certainly* not in our young years.

The father always looked up the road, because he always expected his son to come back. They didn't quarrel or fall out, and his daddy loved him dearly. Then one day, when he had finished working in the field, he looked up and he saw what seemed a familiar speck on the horizon.

To fill out the parable of the Lost Coin into a Black Bible story would take many more details. One might assign the housewife a half month's household budget or income—perhaps she has just cashed her husband's check—and then she loses a tenth of it. The husband's income and attitude would be good to know, and we can visualize the number of rooms swept, the furniture moved, and quality of light by which she searched. Above all, the Black preacher would portray the anxiety and suspense of the housewife—what poor family can stand to lose *any* amount of money! In the end he would relieve the suspense created by the finding of the lost bill. Perhaps it had blown off the kitchen table and under the refrigerator. He would then describe briefly the way the word passed over the back fence or down the street and the neighborhood celebration over the recovery.

This may raise the question in the mind of some as to what right one has to put all these details in when they are not in the Bible. How can one be sure he is not changing or outright destroying God's message? The

Black folk artist using biblical materials may seldom, if ever, consciously verbalize the answers to this question, but they are easy.

In the first place, the story should include, without alteration, every possible aspect of the Bible account. Thus the value of the loss of funds in the parable of the Lost Coin is fixed at a tenth of the total cash on hand for the simple reason that Jesus' version had her losing one of ten coins. The fact that the loss was great enough to warrant a celebration, coupled with the factor of one tenth, suggests that in modern terms the cash on hand must have been equal to a half-month pay check in a one-income family. The wind-blown bill is substituted for the rolling of a coin because no modern coin would loom so large in a family's budget or its recovery warrant a celebration.

In addition to this technical faithfulness to the original account, it is fair to say that the augmented version is (with all the imagination required) a truer and more understandable rendition of the original than the two- or three-verse edition. The great probability is that Jesus himself told such details or the parable would not have survived in the oral tradition. It would not be normal for a terse, flat account to be remembered even a few days, and certainly not for several generations. The written account, then, is a condensation which requires reconstitution, just like dried milk or dehydrated soup if one is to have a full meal.

Finally, the gospel is *preaching* material, not systematic history. This implies proclamation, interpretation or hermeneutic, and understanding in depth. Complete understanding is impossible without a supply of living details out of which to draw meaning, and with which to relate experience. The Bible storyteller has to move in and live in the story before his hearers can do so. The details of all human existence are such that it is hardly possible with these rules and insights to miss the faithful imparting of the real point of the gospel, although that point may well be missed with the mere repetition of the original Bible narrative.

Good storytelling, Black or otherwise, biblical or nonbiblical, requires a sense of timing. The teller must give enough details and action to keep the story moving and compel attention. Yet he must also measure his pace so that the story is understood and the hearer stays abreast of the action in his identification with the narrative. This is especially true in the Black sermon, where the object is very definitely not confined to making sure people know what happened. Black Bible stories are to be relived, not merely heard. This requires a certain expertise in timing and emphasis so that attention is not distracted on the one hand by the effort to keep up or by boredom on the other.

The Rev. George Weaver [6] offered the following story in one of his sermons. In addition to the suspense generated by the action in the narrative, he was able to arouse interest and sustain it through a careful buildup

[6] Pastor of the New Mount Olive Baptist Church of Fort Lauderdale, Fla., preaching at Kansas City, Mo., in the 1969 Annual Session of the National Baptist Convention, U.S.A., Inc.

to Jesus' answer to the question of how to respond to human failure and the violation of an important moral code:

At Jesus' feet is an adulterous woman. She is lying there in the dust of shame and guilt. Standing over her, stones in hand, ready to be judge, jury, and executioner, stand her accusers. I can imagine that one might have had under his arm a scroll, and he had rolled it to Deuteronomy. But he looked at the Master and said, "O man of Galilee, it says here on the scroll that a woman caught as this woman was is to be stoned to death! But tell me, O man of Galilee, you who have walked our streets talking about forgiveness, you who have spoken so eloquently of love, tell me what do you say we should do with her?"

At this juncture, Jesus began to relate to the problem. As a matter of fact, he got down where the problem was. And there with his finger, he began to write in the sand. Now someone said to me that he was stalling for time. I don't think he had to. I rather believe what my grandfather used to say about it—that as he wrote with his finger in the sand, he was saying to the woman's accusers: "Speak not to me about 'It is law,' for this is *the finger* that *wrote* the law on Sinai. Don't tell me what Moses said, because Moses said nothing but what I authorized him to say!" [Great response.]

I don't know why he wrote in the sand. But then he stood up, and took the problem that they had hurled at him and made of it a verbal boomerang and sent it back as a new problem to *them:* the problem of their own *guilt* and their own *conscience.* He said, "He that is without sin, the one of you who is so ready to cast a stone, let him that has perfectly clean hands—let him who can look down the annals of his past and find no guilt—let him whose sheet and record is perfectly plain, cast the *first* stone!"

Then he got back down where the problem was and began to write in the sand. After a while he asked the woman, "Where are your accusers?" The woman said, "I have none." He said, "Neither do I, and I forgive you!"

Now, let us note that he did not condone her sin. He did not compromise with what she had done. And this *must* be the attitude of the church toward *all* immorality! I don't care what you dress it up in—we *must* call it what it is! I can see the woman as she started off—and Jesus said, "*Not yet!* I have not yet dismissed you! I don't want you to leave here believing that I am in accord with what you've done. I must identify what you've done as what it is. Go thy way and sin no more!" I think a person must call it what it is, as we cannot afford to sit idly by and in any way condone wrong. Here we have the pattern set forth by Jesus . . . as to how the church must deal with immorality and sin.

There is considerable imagination used here in supplying detail. There are also some clever theological asides. But all of it is in place. The problem raised at the beginning of the story is not resolved until the end. The punch is not telegraphed. The interest is sustained, because there has been no violation of sequence and no undue eagerness to divulge the conclusion. In the lengthier Bible stories often found in Black sermons, this principle is followed instinctively.

The question may be raised as to why this rule

should be so important when almost everybody has known all his life what the end of the story will be. The answer is implied by the hymns which voice the request to hear the "old, old story over and over again." People want to hear it, not to get to the end and hear the answer, but to relive the experience that leads to the resolution of the conflict. The hearer would hardly verbalize it this way, but he asks to hear the story because he gains new insight and inspiration from each new speaker's way of leading him through the experience. Or he wants to hear a favorite preacher tell it once again, because in each telling he catches fresh measures of meaning as he is led along the old paths he has come to know and love. To break out of sequence and go to the end before finishing the middle is to destroy the beauty of the experience by relegating it to the level of the intellect—away from the realm of the spirit.

The rule of timing not only forbids early disclosure of the climax of the story; it also forbids anticlimax, or lengthy conclusion after the suspense has been relieved. No doubt every storyteller knows this rule, but the Black storyteller of the Biblical narrative has probably arrived at the rule by a completely different route from that taken by others. This is likely to be especially true in the absence of formal training. The Black preacher is in constant dialogue with his audience, and he knows enough not to wear it out when he has let a story unfold to the full. He feels the release of tension and he intuits the loss in interest. So, without any of the rules learned from a textbook or from any formal explanation of the art, he knows it's time to quit or move on to something else.

Through all of this consideration of timing, the principle of spontaneity must still prevail. The orderly progress to a logical climax is not a function of careful editing or following the manual. Such techniques might help a formally trained Black preacher in his preparation; but no story can live if it is read from a paper. So timing in actual delivery must be a spontaneous product of the dialogue.

The parallel of a performance in another art may be instructive here. A Black musician practices faithfully, but he never plays a selection exactly the same way twice. Nor would he sing a solo the same way twice. A Soul singer in the Black idiom would engage in still greater variety of improvisations. All of these artists would follow a pattern of free rendition from memory of the basic themes or structures. The authenticity of such a free rendition more than offsets any losses incurred from lack of musical score, so the artist has what might be called the courage of his imperfections. He knows that the losses from a slavish adherence to every minor technicality on paper would be far greater than the losses from a free rendition from memory. Yet, he knows that preparation and practice are extremely helpful.

So it is with the art of telling Bible stories in the Black idiom. As I have said, every additional archaeological detail helps feed the Black imagination. And reading and prewriting (including timing) may be helpful to some. But when the story is told, it must be told freely and directly to be effective or to be worthy of the Black tradition of storytelling in the pulpit.

I think it might help sum up what I have said about imaginative detail, timing, plot, goals, et cetera, to present two Black renditions of parables which have been taken from tapes of sermons I preached in 1966. They were addressed to a small congregation engaged in a church conflict where there was a great need to be able to forgive:

The Parable of the Unforgiving Servant [7]

What Jesus has taught us to do is to make rules that we can apply to other folks and ourselves with equal ease. If any of you want to set laws about *him* without looking at what *you* are doing, you may discover, to your utter chagrin, that those laws will cut *you* up worse than they'll cut him up.

Jesus told a story of a man who had perhaps been a bookkeeper for the king, and he stole, he absconded, he misplaced a million or more dollars—it could have been as much as ten million dollars in today's money. I don't know whether he had expensive girlfriends, or played the horses with it or what, but it was gone—all gone! Then one day the king had his books audited and the cover was pulled off. By this time the king was pretty upset. He was hot with that bookkeeper. He called that rascal in and ordered him—his wife and the whole family—to be sold for a small part payment.

But the man stood up in front of the king and pled and cried and pled and just carried on so. . . . Talking 'bout,

[7] Matthew 18:23–35.

"Give me a break, I'll pay you every cent." And the king said to himself, "Well, if I did put him in jail, I'd just be feeding him. And there's no way in the world a *working* man could start to pay the *interest,* much less pay back the principal; and I could hardly miss the price they'd bring on the slave market. No man in his right mind would *ever* let him keep books again."

So he let him go—forgave the scoundrel! Happy now, this dude fell down before the king and thanked him and kissed his feet and all that. O happy day!

In no time the bookkeeper went out in the street and he met another servant that owed him a measly two dollars, just enough for one bet on a horse at the race-track. And the Bible tells us that he grabbed him by the throat like this [gestures—grabbing both coat lapels with one hand near the throat] and said, "Looka here, man, I want mah money, and I want it *now!*" The poor fella fell down on his knees and pled for patience. He promised to pay it all just as soon as he could. But the king's ex-book-keeper wouldn't hear to it at all. He called a sheriff and had his old friend thrown in jail.

One of the king's servants was passing in the meantime and saw the whole thing. He couldn't get to the king fast enough. "Your majesty, you know what? You just gave that rascal a million dollars, and he's out there tryin' to throw his friend in jail for two measly bucks."

Let me tell you, the king got mad. He was furious. He said, "Send him back in here." And when he came in, the king said, "Put him *under* the jail and throw the key away!" Because you see, the measure that he used on his two-dollar debtor was the same measure that was used on him; only for him it was a lot *harder* than it was on his friend.

Whatever you use to measure your friends and fellow members, God is gonna send for you to come back and say, "Looka, here, Sister, looka here Brother, if you gonna be this rough, how will it fit on *you?*"

The Parable of the Wheat and the Tares [8]

Jesus tells a story of some men who went out for their master and sowed wheat. And when they put the wheat out, it—it began to grow—they discovered there were a lot of other things coming up among the wheat. And they worried about this thing and they went to him and they said, "Look, didn't we put *good* seed in the ground? What's goin' on here?" And the master said, "You know, one of my enemies must have sowed tares in my field. He didn't want me to prosper." The men said, "Well, that devilish fellow has sure been out here making it rough. Shall we go out and weed the wheat?" And the master said, "No, wait a minute! You know you can't tell so easily the difference between wheat and tares."

And I know what he meant! When I went to Fresno, we planted a yard, and all of those little green things started to coming up. And I couldn't tell goat-heads from grass to save my neck; at first they all looked just alike. The master said, "Don't you go out there and try to pull up the tares, because you can't tell the difference. You aren't smart enough to see which one is which. And if you go out there pulling up tares, you may pull up some good wheat." He said, "I tell you what I want you to do. I want you to let 'em grow together! And when they get all the way up and ready for the harvest, *I'll* separate them! Don't you *worry* yourself about separating them;

[8] Matthew 13:25–30.

I'll separate them. And when I separate them, they'll be separated *right!"*

We have to learn that it is not for us to judge *who* is wheat and *who* is tares—*who* is in God's church and *who* of us ought be out. It's *all* of them in there *together*. We're all sinners saved by grace! If anybody is still a rank sinner, let *him* separate them; don't let us even meddle with that. We are not sharp enough to separate them. We've got to be careful. We have no license to judge and no license to separate.

VI

Black English

Black preaching requires the use of Black language—the rich rendition of English spoken in the Black ghetto. To many Americans, of whatever color, such an assertion may cause some consternation. People will ask, "Do you want me to say 'dis and dat'?" or "Must I unlearn all my learning and talk 'flat'?" This raises three important questions: 1.) Why Black English in the first place? 2.) How is it learned? 3.) And what is Black English anyway? I shall try to resolve them in the order given.

The not-very-well-known-fact about all spoken English is that there is no one universally accepted or "proper" version. "Standard" American English, to the extent that there is a version more generally accepted than others, is probably a North-Midland white, middle-class variety of English. Every other region of the U.S.A. will have its own variant of this speech standard, even within the same middle-class white majority.

Every ethnic group or regional subculture will have its variants, each peculiarly conditioned by the influences of history, geography, social class, and the like.

Such groups are sometimes referred to as speech communities. Within such a speech community it is easiest to communicate by using the language of that group. The subtle meaning and shades of meaning, the particular pronunciation and accent, the intonation and total signal system of any given group are altogether "proper" to that group. In fact, no language is improper among its own users, since it alone is most capable of the task for which all language exists: communication.

This rule is especially meaningful to missionaries in foreign lands. They take great care to learn the communication system of the people among whom they are to work. However, in America, a diabolical combination of racism, class snobbery, and naïveté has caused Blacks as well as whites to assume, consciously or unconsciously, that there is a single proper American English, and that the language spoken by most Black people is a crude distortion of it. In religious circles, standard white middle-class English is assumed to be the only vehicle for the preaching of the gospel and the praising of the Lord in public. The results have been rather disastrous for the church of the Black masses, because the vast majority of Black-culture churches have found it difficult to understand or relate to trained Black clergymen preaching whiteese to them. Consequently, those trained Blacks who are also fluent in Black English—the language of their people—are conspicuously effective and in great demand.

It is true that Black clergymen have had to be, for the most part, white-culture proficient in order to satisfy college and seminary requirements. But then American colleges and seminaries are heavily conditioned by the not-so-subtle assumption that "white is right," especially the white, middle-class culture and its language.

The result is that, when a substantial number of Black-culture churches have been faced with the choice between a pastor who could communicate with them or a man who was merely educated, they have chosen communication over education. In fact, it has often been argued by the faithful that those preachers who deliberately tried to preach white to their Black congregations were possibly not even "saved." The sincerest efforts of trained men to relate themselves to the Black-ghetto church have accordingly been misunderstood at times. Their efforts have been tainted by their unconscious lack of the cultural integrity which is crucial to Black identity. To lose one's language is to lose one's identity. To refuse to learn and use the people's language is an affront to the people one presumes to serve. The new breed of truly educated Black clergymen has been lately awakened to the subtleties of this impasse, and they are doing something about it. While it may still be embarrassing to the educated Black seminarian, who is still conditioned by the presumptions of the white middle class, it is rewarding for others who have learned to come to terms with their heritage to have it whispered around the churches that "the pastor's finally got religion!"

On the other hand, some Black churches have pastors whose fluency is limited to the Black idiom. Because they feel themselves limited, such pastors often avoid contact beyond their home churches and their own culture. As a result, their churches may forfeit involvement in issues or programs which are relevant to many needs of the Black man today. Their limited effectiveness creates a vacuum or a distortion in ghetto leadership, and the Black community may be divorced from the larger influence of the church.

One answer to this problem lies in teaching pastors who are already fluent in Black exposition to be at home in standard English, so that they can increase their capacities to deal with issues. Another answer lies in the teaching of Black language and religious culture to the professionally trained Black clergy, who may then make more effective use of their training and deal more effectively with the needs of the Black masses and the issues affecting their well-being. Still a third answer lies in the recruitment of able Black-culture-oriented candidates for training in the seminaries, carefully avoiding brainwashing them or stripping them of their original culture. All too many theological seminaries have been in the habit of molding Blacks into a white image and sending them out to serve Black people in Black churches. And this unfortunate practice is not limited to seminaries that are white. But the rigidity of these white-oriented seminaries is diminishing somewhat, and a new generation of Blacks is being permitted to discover the beauty of being what they are—Black.

The question will no doubt arise as to why the church is not used to convey standard culture and "lift" the Black masses into the mainstream of the American culture and its benefits. The answer is very simple: no free Black-culture church will ever call a pastor who cannot speak the language of its people. To expect them to become bicultural may be realistic. But to expect them to learn their cultural duality from a Black white man is absurd. Neither faith nor culture will be communicated by a preacher whose language sounds to the ghetto resident as if he is putting on airs, for implicit in his posturing is a deprecation of the people he wants to serve. His rejection will be summary if it is sensed that his fundamental loyalties are to his white reference group rather than to the religious culture of his own people.

The seminary-trained Black must be a model of all things to all men, helping the cultures to come closer together by being an instrument of translation of each to the other. He must be fluent in Black language, for this is fundamental to his calling, and yet he must also be fluent in standard English, because he must communicate beyond his congregation. His language must be Black enough to generate confidence in an identity which is clearly Black. He must be able to reach the souls of Black folk with Soul language, putting them at ease and gaining maximum access by avoiding all the linguistic signals of social distance from his congregation. Yet he must also be able to reinforce and keep alive the language learnings of the young people of his congregation which link them to the larger community.

He must assure his congregation that he doesn't talk flat all the time, so that they will have confidence that he can adequately represent their interests outside the ghetto.

This type of bilingual skill has been resisted by middle-class teachers in the Black ghetto, on the grounds that it is phony and seems to make fun of the ghetto culture as a setting for an Amos-and-Andy set of mannerisms. If Black language were suggested as the sole vehicle of spoken communication, then of course the protesting teachers would seem to have a point. Even so, Black language is far more than an ignorant jumble of unaspirated mumbling. It is the lingua franca of the Black ghetto, full of subtle shadings of sound and significance, cadences and color. It beguiles the hearer because it is familiar. It establishes rapport with him and influences him, without his being conscious of the fact that the preacher has deliberately chosen the language most appropriate to his task of meaningful communication. This is one of the chief skills of the Black preacher who is effective and charismatic despite his white-oriented professional training. The cadences of the late Dr. Martin Luther King, Jr., were unashamedly Black. His learning could be used to lead the Black masses because he was always heard as a Soul Brother.

Before offering some technical description and analysis of the Black language presently in wide use, I should perhaps explain, as far as possible, how this language is learned. All languages are learned best by living and identifying with the people who speak them. In a sense, one must for a time burn his bridges and identify solely with the target culture group. When this is done, the language will be learned subconsciously. Thus children reproduce the speech of those socially closest to them (family and peer group) rather than those whom they may hear most—e.g., teacher or television. Should the family change neighborhoods and encounter a difference between their speech and the speech of the child's new playmates, the child's choice of identity will be subconsciously decided, but that choice will become evident through his choice of speech patterns. The preacher who grew up with white speech will best learn Black speech after he has overcome the subtle vestiges of the white self-identity that went with his white tongue. To be sure, he may need to retain some whiteness in order to be truly bicultural and bilingual. But if he is to talk Black, and if he hopes to reach Blacks effectively, he will have to become a person of primarily Black identity. Given an acceptance and appreciation of Black identity, one's ear is attuned to the sounds of one's folks, and one's tongue consciously and subconsciously shapes its own sounds to avoid contrast with those to whom one feels closest. The more unconscious and therefore not self-conscious the Black utterance is, the better the possibilities of perfect communication.

The Black preacher might well develop a range of situations in which he employs degrees of Blackness in utterance. For example, a sermon or conversation might include a quote of extremely Black speech in such a way as not to ridicule the original speaker and, in fact, to interpret that person more accurately. In another situation, one might deal rather analytically with a matter in the pure standard dialect. In still another situation, one might paraphrase a verse of scripture. For instance, a Black preacher might render God's speech to Peter in the text against racism (Acts 10:14–15): "Looka here, Peter, don't you be callin' *nothin'* I made common or dirty!"

This, of course, requires the Black intonation and accent so necessary to the complete Black signal system, but the Blackness of such a translation must, in some measure, come through on even the black and white of this paper. It has several important advantages. In the first place it presents the message in a familiar and authentic folk-art form, and attracts attention by giving pleasure and making folks at home or comfortable. Secondly, it reinforces and supports Black identity by putting in the mouth of God the language of the people. In white-language preaching this highly important emotional support is reserved for members of the white-speech community. No Black man can truly identify with a God who speaks only the language of the white oppressor. A Black rendition of scripture does in language what a Black Christ or a Black Madonna does in art. God is divested of his "proper," white, socially distant role, a personification of deity completely outside Black culture and life. Just how great is this need for reidentification of God with Black people can be seen in the words of a prayer by a faithful Black deacon: "If your blue eyes in glory find anything wrong in this place . . ."

Finally, the message is made much more understandable by the use of familiar language. The lesson of the message is better learned because the scene is experienced in the worship rather than simply heard in theory. The experience factor is greatly reduced when the message is offered in a foreign tongue.

The progress here discussed is parallel to the changes of language and image now being developed in textbooks for Black ghetto schools across the country. Just as the language of the "Dick and Jane" readers gets minimal response from the Black-ghetto child (and has therefore to be discarded), so must total dependence on white middle-class language be translated for effective Black-ghetto preaching, and for the same reasons. In fact, if a preacher uses standard English exclusively with no Black sounds and shadings, the chances of his being asked back to a Black-culture church are not great. It goes without saying that his chances of receiving a call to pastor such a church are virtually nil. The rejection of the preacher will not be a rejection of his education per se, but a resistance to the imposition of a different culture on an institution that is Black owned and Black controlled, and can therefore insist on being led by a Black pastor.

What then are the contrasting features which distinguish Black English from standard English? One is the slower rate of delivery. Another is Black sentence structure, which on the average is simpler than white middle-class sentence structure. Still other differences range all the way from highly technical and subtle usages down to the peculiar tonal inflections characteristic of Southern Blacks. As I have said, no book about these speech features could teach one to use them effectively. The best that can be done in a book is to describe them. Only a healthily Black identity, born of acute exposure to the Black experience and of complete Black self-acceptance, can complete the process of lingual identification and implant Black language naturally on one's tongue.

Perhaps the commonest feature stereotypically associated with Black speech is the "down home" drawl, which must not be confused with the white Southern drawl from the same region. The Black drawl is accompanied by "flatness," a word denoting lazily articulated vowels and consonants, and imprecise closure or dropped word endings. This description must not be taken as a white-standard judgment against Black language or culture. It is simply a fact that the word "lazy" applies to both Black and white Southern pronunciation of the long vowel "I." It is composed of "ah" and "ee," and both give only the first part. But the whites probably drop it more than Blacks, either North or South. In fact, the first Black President of the United States will probably have to sound much more standard on his long "I" vowels than did the first President from Texas, who was white.

If one can forget the negative connotations of lazy speech, one can sense that soft velvet sounds have a much greater capacity to communicate warmth and avoid harsh overtones. Few can deny the charm of a drawl. Many Southern whites go so far as to consider it an identity signal of Southern aristocracy. Whatever fear Blacks have of a drawl, as used by whites, has been conditioned not by the sound itself but by the racist treatment that has all too often gone with it. In a word, the softened consonants have universal advantage and signal value in the Black speech community. The degree of softening may vary greatly, but Blackese is surely not characterized by crisp consonants.

A full-fledged drawl, however, is obviously not by any means a universal characteristic of Black speech. Neither is another feature: unmatched subjects and verbs. This failure of agreement between subjects and verbs is called bad grammar, and it may be so within the white middle-class communication system. But the word "bad" must never be used by one culture regarding another. No language is bad which conveys adequately the intended meaning to the intended audience. "Ungrammatical" is a less judgmental term, but it still implies that there is one form which is standard, by which all others are judged. Among Blacks of the ghetto, the speaker does not have to say "You is" to be accepted, but he is certainly permitted to say it if he wishes, and many will not hear anything wrong about it. "You is" *and* "you are" are permitted in the Black mother tongue.

Much good communication takes place in Black culture without such extreme contrasts with white language as "You is." One can be quite Black and still use neither a drawl nor such bad grammar as "He play the piano." Perhaps the most important thing is that a Black hears departures from white standard English and has no urge to correct them, because he has lost all desire to please the white man with his own speech.

Another interesting contrast between Blackese and standard speech is in the different uses to which Blacks put function words or prepositions. When one says in Blackese "I got sick behind it," he means after it in time and not behind it in space. Blacks sang "Freedom over Me" in slavery days, and young Blacks popularized the slave song in the sit-in era, but the word "over" designated no relationship normally associated with the preposition "over" in white speech. Then there is the common Black statement "I'm gonna go up side your head." It means, "I'm going to hit you on the head." It implies two prepositions, "up" and "beside," but here again is a wide and common departure from standard usage. A final illustration is the word "around." To "mess around" is colloquial for aimless or nonproductive activity. But in Blackese the usage is altered to give the verb "mess" a direct object. It is common to hear a Black complain, "You messed me round."

It is not mandatory that a Black use this language, but it never hurts. A Black English teacher in a high school told me recently of a noisy back row of Blacks who simply would not join the class. When she departed from the script and sternly declared, "Y'all ain't talkin' 'bout nothin'!" they sat up and took notice. This was her opening wedge of communication.

Another common contrast with standard English involves archaic English and logical but ungrammatical constructions. One of these is quoted above in God's response to Peter. "Don't you be callin' . . ." is a logical combination, but the grammatical or accepted way to say it in whitese is "Don't you dare call . . ." This same irregular verb "to be" is treated by Blacks as a regular verb and a report on a person's condition may be rendered "He be's all right." An archaic pronunciation of the auxiliary verb "might" survives in a common response in Black lodge ritual as they intone: "So mote it be." And it survives as "mought" (rhymes with "out") in the conversation of Blacks from Virginia and North Carolina. Blacks also use words like "fetch," "tote," "holp" (for "help"), and "yonder," to a greater extent than other groups. But all these usages can be found among whites, particularly Appalachian whites.

It may be argued on the basis of this shared vocabulary that language differences are regional rather than racial. But, as has been pointed out already, there is a considerable difference between white Southern dialect and Blackese. Regional influences will indeed be shared between Black and white, but the major influence on Black culture and language is the Black experience, and this is not shared with whites. The Black man lives in another world from the white man of the same Southern city. And the racial aspect of cultural difference only increases in the North, where white Southerners are assimilated or at least distributed, and Blacks from the South are huddled together to cling to their beleaguered dignity and their mother tongue. Blackese will mean far more to a Northern-born resident of the ghetto than Southernese would mean to an ex-Southern white, simply because the white man can literally be assimilated and the Black cannot.

However, even with the easy adjustment of whites among whites, the rule that all men love to hear their mother tongue is illustrated by the popularity among whites of Hillbilly or Country and Western music, a part of whose charm is the dialect. Affluent whites, as well as deprived white migrants, like to hear the way people spoke "when I was a kid." Blacks whose natural inclinations have not been destroyed will follow the rule also. The native language is comforting to all who have not denied their roots and identity.

This indicates something very significant to the educated Black clergyman, about how he must be linguistically flexible in order to communicate with all of his congregation at all times and in all circumstances. In times of crisis especially, no man hears well the words of a stranger spoken in a foreign tongue. To communicate effectively the Black preacher has to adjust his language to a variety of contexts and many shadings within the two basic cultures, Black and white. The most crucial of his contexts is the Black pulpit, and the most demanding culture for his purposes is Blackamerican, in contrast with what is considered standard or white middle class.

VII

The Black Style

From its earliest beginnings Black preaching has been clearly characterized by great emphasis on personal style or individual variations. About the most certain statement one can make about Black preaching style is that *nothing* is certain or fixed. Styles of Black preachers range all the way from those known to proclaim the gospel from ladders and coffins and in other spectacular ways, to others noted for standing "flat-footed" or in one place and hardly raising their voices, while stirring large audiences. In between is a vast array of mannerisms, styles, and approaches well worth reviewing, both because of human interest and because of their influence on the communication of the gospel in the Black-culture church.

The first thing that must be said about unusual mannerisms is that the Black congregation is very permissive. It accepts a considerable variety of behavior unrelated to the message, in order (consciously or unconsciously) to free preachers to be themselves. One preacher in wide demand among Blacks and whites pops his suspenders when he is really caught up in his message, and free. Another unbuttons his collar and seems to dig his chin into his chest. Another has exclaimed for years, "Bless my bones!" Still another starts his sermons only after an unbelievably long, intense, and even stern glare at the congregation. Black-culture Christians tend to enjoy mannerisms, provided they are natural and not overworked. They add interest and signal a freedom and authentic personhood in which the congregation participates vicariously. The Black-culture preacher does not have to develop a striking mannerism or trademark in order to be accounted Black, but it certainly is not a handicap if he happens to engage in strange and colorful action peculiar to himself alone. Individuality is celebrated, and acceptance is communicated by the congregation in a way enjoyed by all who have not bowed the knee to the Baal of white conformity.

In addition to mannerisms Black preachers abound in other stylistic features. The most common or stereotypical is the use of a musical tone or chant in preaching. Among the initiates it is variously referred to as "moaning," "mourning," "whooping," "tuning," "zooning," or any one of several other terms, each with a slightly different shade of meaning.

Sustained tone is used in various ways. Some Black preachers use it only in climactic utterance, of whatever length. Others, often less well-educated and therefore less inhibited, tend to use some degree of tone throughout the message. Still others use it only in places where the culture of the congregation clearly demands it. The decision will often be made unconsciously, just as a truck driver adjusts his gears to fit the demands of the road. Yet most churches do not demand tone, so that the present significance of this feature is very difficult to assess beyond the fact that it automatically makes some folks "happy" just to hear this aspect of their mother tongue sounded in the pulpit. For people with a certain background, it appears that a moaned message is more deeply spiritual than an unintoned one. While this is not necessarily true, tone does signal a kind of affirmation of Black identity which in turn begets a real religious experience. Another way to say it would be that for many older Blacks their first religious experience came with intoned preaching; thereafter the response became more and more conditioned, so that any preacher using such a technique would automatically get a greater response.

Historically speaking, intonation as a factor in Black preaching style no doubt stems from the African custom of singing almost everything. The history of much of Black Africa was preserved, in the absence of writing, in song. So were laws, customs and traditional folk stories and hero tales. There were also highly spontaneous or impromptu songs for various life situations, such as the voicing of grievances. And there were folktales or fables of wisdom and morality, for guidance in life's problems.[1] This understanding of history and an-

---

[1] Fisher, *Negro Slave Songs in the United States*, pp. 1–13.

thropology add much to the accuracy of our knowledge of the very first Negro spirituals, as contrasted with those edited and published later. It also explains why early Black peddlers (and some to this day) sold ice, coal, fish, and vegetables with street-chanted sales talks, and why Black crowds thronged to hear a message moaned or intoned.[2] What once took the place of print in African culture stayed on to serve Blacks in other ways. It reminded them of home at first, and later it was simply something they had to themselves, not shared with or understood or controlled by whites. It was an affirmation of Black identity, a means of celebrating and supporting Black personhood.

While intonation has general significance as an identity signal, it has certainly come to be used widely by Black preachers to indicate inspirational climax or the end of the message. Yet intonation seemed seldom to be taken seriously by acknowledged leaders of the Black pulpit, as indicated by a study of tapes of Black preaching which I carried out. Only a few seemed really to depend on it. In more than half, the moaning climax was not sustained or apparently important. This was especially true of the most effective preachers.

In fact, although three fourths of the more widely known preachers I studied used some form of tone in their inspirational climaxes, a highly significant minority of equal impact used nothing of the sort. Further, I found that, while some of these speakers did not use intonation on any of the tapes in my collection, they

[2] *Ibid.*, p. 17.

did use it on other occasions. It was readily apparent that many Black congregations no longer require intonation for a religiously climactic experience. The more universal factor seemed to be climactic material. Some of this amounted to old, well-worn climax clichés. Among the preachers whom I considered the better ones, climax material tended to be related to the solid content of the message, while at the same time being inherently moving as well as movingly presented.

Perhaps the most important thing that can be said about intonation is that it can never be used effectively unless it is the natural style of language of the speaker. To use it insincerely as an easy means of access and manipulation is to run the risk of failure as well as to belittle and degrade the Black preaching tradition. But it should also be said that, wherever pastors or congregations frown on and repress this common feature of Black religious culture, the worship is no longer in the idiom of the Black masses. For Black worship, the warm acceptance of any manifestation of the Black experience sincerely used must be taken for granted.

Closely associated with the stereotypical use of tone by Black preachers is the use of rhythm in preaching. Most white observers, including folklorists as well as anthropologists and theologians, never seem to be able to discover the one without the other. However, my own observations of thirty years in the pulpit as well as my study of tapes would seem not to give much support to the idea that Black preachers use rhythm to any great degree. The most that could be said about the vast majority of preachers I have studied is that lengthy intonation requires breaks for breath! In many cases, this makes room for response, but it is not usually at meaningful places, nor does it seem to follow anything like a poetic or musical beat or rhythm.

It would be safe to say, I think (as I have already said of mannerisms and of tone), that modern Black worshippers do not require or expect any special pattern or rhythm. If a Black preacher happens to have a rhythmic singsong delivery, it is, like other features, warmly accepted so long as it appears sincere. For a few it may be a pleasant reminder of older days when it may have been much more common. Among some sects it is used for a mass rhythmic experience which may or may not be truly religious. For the rest, my studies would seem to indicate that, while rhythm is vitally important in Black music, it is, to say the least, unimportant in Black preaching.

A far more important feature, implied in the consideration of rhythm, is the call-and-response pattern. Many preachers who pause momentarily for breathing or other reasons receive a response from the audience. When a Black preacher quotes the centurion (Matthew 27:54), it is almost obligatory that he pause after the first "truly" and wait for the congregation to repeat the word. In fact, this may be done several times before the quotation (excellent for climax) is completed with "this was the Son of God." This pattern has roots deep in Black African culture.

The Black preacher who is still uneasy and inhibited about such worship techniques as this call-and-response should remember that even the cold liturgy of the white church gives people a place in the Collects or series of prayers! How much better, for purposes of Black worship, to provide in the sermon a place where Black people can express themselves or unburden their hearts with a "Have mercy!" or "Truly!" or "Early!" Here is genuine, happy, satisfying dialogue with the preacher. Nowhere is there a better example of the audience participation now so suddenly treasured, in theory at least, by whites.

In truly Black preaching, repetition occurs not only in the call-and-response pattern, but in the normal course of the sermon. Texts, aphorisms, and other significant statements are restated for emphasis, memory, impact and effect. The Black audience takes the gospel seriously and does not feel talked down to when words or sentences are repeated. Not uncommonly, repetition is so vivid that it may be heard again in later conversation, days after it was given life in the pulpit. If the gospel is indeed the word of life, ought it not to include nuggets worth repeating the next day or the next year? Black preaching assumes that things need time to sink in. The emphasis is on intensity of response and not extensity of material covered. What in another context might seem pompous becomes meaningful in the Black congregation where repetition has a completely different connotation.

Black preachers, like any others, risk pomposity when they assume roles in their speaking—like the role of God or of some other character or spectator in a Bible narrative—but a role carefully portrayed is a tremendous asset to preaching. Every Black-culture

Christian has heard a preacher say, "I saw John—on the Isle of Patmos—*early* one Sunday morning. . . ." Whatever the role or multiplicity of roles assumed, it adds immeasurably to the impact and value of the story. The Black preacher who is so "siditty" [3] as to preach always in the third person is clearly not Black-culture—and not effective. The Black preacher who combines imagination with role playing and spontaneous dramatization can hardly fail to reach, hold, and lift his Black audience.

Related to role playing is the common and very creative custom of using the best folk storytelling techniques. Characterizations are sometimes elaborately worked out. The details used give the audience many ways to identify with and learn from the experience of the character in the story. The following story from a sermon by Dr. S. M. Lockridge [4] is a good illustration of this type of detail and congregational identification:

> As they went up to the temple to pray, a certain man—don't know this man's name, but the next few words tell us somewhat of his condition—a certain man that was lame from his mother's womb. When it said "a lame man," that made me feel sorry for him because it is a pitiful thing when a man has been useful and now has lost his usefulness. He has become lame and not able to get around.
>
> But when I got to thinking about this man who was lame, and I remember the writer said that he was lame

[3] A Blackese word meaning "sedate," with a connotation of pretense or middle-class striving.

[4] Pastor, Calvary Baptist Church, San Diego, Cal.

from his mother's womb, that made it all the more pitiful to me. For not only was he a lame man, but he had been lame all his life. And I can think of nothing more pitiful than a lame baby—one who was born into the world and whose parents have ever hoped some day he will be strong and healthy. I can see those parents watching him day in and day out, but he never had any use of his limbs. He grew old in age, but still lame.

I think it was last fall, or some time recently, a teen-ager was told that one of his legs would have to be amputated. He just hated the idea. "Here I am a teen-ager, where all of the other children my age are active in getting around, doing this and that; and conditions are such that I will have to lose one of my legs and be a cripple the rest of my life." You remember he tried to run away from home because he didn't want his leg amputated.

Well, it is a pitiful thing to see a teen-ager lame. But, here, this man had *never* been able to use his limbs, and had been lame from his mother's womb. This man had to be carried. You know we can understand this man's condition because he couldn't help himself. I know a lot of people in the church that are healthy and strong but they still want to be carried. . . . They had to carry this man and they brought him daily and laid him at a gate called Beautiful. Now they carried him daily, it means that he must have been receiving something that kept him coming back. . . . Look at that man that was made by the hands of God. That man is lame and twisted, and had to be carried.

Well, when he saw Peter and John going into the temple, he got glad because, you know, he had begged so long until he could just look at a person as he approached and he could tell what kind of gift he was going to get. I can understand, somehow, how he felt. At one time I used to hop bells at a hotel. And, you know, after a few years I could look at a guest when he pulled up in front of the door and I could pretty well tell what kind of a tip I was going to get. Oh, I could look at his bags, yes, I could . . . I could look at the way he was dressed and I could tell the type, the size of tip I was going to get.

Well, this man had been in the business so long until he could look and size up the kind of gift he was going to get. But this time he underestimated. Yes, he did! He knew that he could get a good gift from Peter and John, but he was looking for alms. He was looking for something that he could exchange at the supermarket. Oh, but Peter and John said, "Look on us." And every one of us who is the representative of the Lord ought to be able to tell the world to "look on us.". . .

The speaker then went on to make the point, finally, that the man was healed in the name and by the power of Jesus.

The Bible abounds in characters about whom such details can be developed for easy identification. In another sermon Dr. Lockridge tells the story of poor man Lazarus with substantial details for the identification of the congregation. In his rendition of the Lazarus story, he heightened the conflict between what might be identified as the good guys and the bad guys with great inventiveness, developing suspense right up to the last moment, when there was, of course, the victory of the good guys. Another preacher led the congregation from locked door to locked door in a jail as an angel delivered Paul. Before this he had spelled out the lack of cash for a bail bondsman for Paul, a very familiar story to the people who live in the Black ghettos and who often find themselves held in the white man's jail on questionable charges.

While these stories were highly entertaining, they were also most effective Black preaching. For the Black preacher, the victory of the good guys is not a cheap, contrived thing. Underneath it all is the clear implication of the final victory of God, justice, and righteousness. For disinherited people, there is no doctrine more essential than this to survival and to remaining creative in one's struggle for liberation.

For the purposes of Black preaching, the conflict is not between good cops and bad robbers, nor is it between heroic Western law men and outlaw cowboys. In fact, it is not a morality play related to any typical middle-class model of virtue. It is the conflict of the powerless with the powerful, the have-nots against the haves. To frame it as the just against the unjust is perhaps the closest possible way to correlate the Black conflict with the standard, white, ethical conflict. As always, the conflict has to be that which is personally crucial to the hearer. Thus, when Professor Cone says that Black theology is the theology of liberation, his facts have historic validity. They are not some recently devised, wishful dreams of a Black scholar in search of applause.

This whole matter of personal involvement also affects the style of the preacher from within. The inner fervor of a preacher has great importance. In Black culture it does not hurt to be one's own best customer, moved by one's own utterance. To be sure, it may seem crude to flaunt, "I'm beginning to feel pretty good now." But the self-contained, conversational tone of the white preacher cannot be maintained by the Black preacher who is caught up in doing God's preaching. A Black preacher has to let himself go. He feels what he is preaching about: freedom, sorrow, fear, rage, and joy. He must make no pretense of so-called objectivity. You can't be objective when God lays his hand on you. You "preach what the Spirit say preach, and you do what the spirit say do!"

The Black congregation responds to beauty of language—the well-turned phrase. This does not mean complexity of structure. In fact Black-culture preachers often use short, easily remembered sentences. But they use rhetorical flair. And the Black deacon also loves to pray in highly poetic language. The flow and phraseology of the King James Version will never die in America while Black Christianity stays Black.

To be sure, there are still some Black as well as white preachers who are brazenly ornate. They pay the price for their linguistic acrobatics by divorcing attention from the point of the sermon, if there be any. In fact it is probable that the present white standard commitment to dour, barren language, offered in the name of simplicity, is a direct reaction to the flowery excesses of many white preachers of a past generation. On the other hand, for Blacks and for many others capable of spiritual warmth, the impact of the lessons of the faith is greatly enhanced by the natural poetry and music of gifted preachers. Dr. Gardner C. Taylor is a case in point. Real Soul preaching demands more rhetorical flair than is "proper" to the middle-class white commitment. This is not to imply that good Black preaching uses rhetoric for a crutch. In fact in my study of Black sermons, rhetoric more often than not was absent from the climactic utterance. Perhaps it would be accurate to say that *one* of the many strengths of good Black preaching is the skillful use of poetic rhetoric.

In the previous chapter I called attention to the slow rate of delivery of most Black preachers. Statistics for a scientific comparison with white preachers do not exist, so far as I know. One difficulty is that the selection of a valid Black sample is complicated by the fact that there are, here and there, accomplished Black preachers with a truly rapid-fire delivery. On the whole, however, it appears unquestionable that most successful Black preaching is done with a significantly lower number of words per minute. The Black preacher takes his time. When he is preaching, there is nothing more important that he could be doing.

This attitude has some interesting implications. One might logically expect that the content of the Black sermon is likely to be scant. Not so. The deliberate speed of the Black preacher can be more than compensated for by the increase in the length of the sermon. Another misconception might be that the preachers have to go slow because they *can't* go fast. Wrong again. The Black preacher measures his delivery to maximize comprehension and influence. Many Black preachers could radically increase the rate without violence to the quality of delivery if circumstances demanded it.

The fundamental significance of the slow rate is comprehension and impact. The intelligent preacher knows that true comprehension is an emotional as well as an intellectual process. Even given a quick mind, the Black hearer needs time for the essence to sink in. No human mind operates by pushed buttons and lightning speed. So the Black preacher slows his rate and deals deliberately with his material to the end that his congregation never has the sense of being rushed.

The Black slave song, or the Negro spiritual, is an interesting parallel to the slow rate characteristic of the Black preaching style. Despite massive, though well-intentioned, meddling with the originals when whites started putting them on paper after the Civil War, the spiritual is still clearly the product of its Black African culture roots, and the Black-culture sermon is the homiletical twin brother to the spiritual. In the case of the sung culture, a whole song can be formed on a very small word base. Haunting choruses are built on as few as four words: "Remember me, O Lord, remember me." Where a white-culture hymn has long stanzas full of words delivered at a fairly rapid rate, a Black spiritual might simply say slowly, "Lord, I want to be a Christian in my heart." The slow rate of Black preaching, as well as the repetition, is the natural pattern of Black speaking and singing, neither of which is prone to depend on great numbers of words in a brief utterance.

There are several lesser stylistic features. One is the

use of aphorisms—clever, pithy statements. While this is fairly common in preaching of all cultures, it would appear that the use of aphorisms is more frequent among the great Black preachers of America. It is also apparent that the response of the Black audience to aphorisms is much greater than is customary in other churches. In the case of two very popular speakers, revival sermons in strange churches were introduced by a whole series of aphorisms. They were extraneous and unrelated to each other, but the response to both preachers was, as intended, the building of excellent rapport with the new congregation. With this warm-up, the preacher could begin the real task of a sermon, certain of the attention of the congregation.

Another lesser feature is the stammer or the hesitation. In addition to building suspense and increasing interest in the ultimate expression to be delivered, this technique seems to portray the preacher as groping for truth, of struggling to hear what is coming from above. This is not altogether limited to Black preaching. However, it does have greater currency in the ghetto where it has the additional effect of avoiding an impression of overwhelming intellect and slick presentation. It gives an image of weakness with which the mostly underdog congregation can sympathize and identify. As the preacher searches and gropes, the members of the congregation cry, "Help him, Lord!" as evidence of their warm identification with the speaker.

It is obvious then that all of these stylistic features have more to commend them than simple habit. The subtle implications of every single feature or mannerism are consciously or unconsciously weighed before that feature becomes a permanent part of the good Black preacher's style. This is true whether the preacher is learned in the formal educational sense or utterly without schooling. The most that I can establish from comparative studies is some evidence that the educational influence increases the range or spectrum of features used by the preacher. Conversely, it is interesting to note that no level of use by a speaker who is not formally trained could be found not to be duplicated by some professionally trained speakers. In other words, the styles of learned and unlearned preachers completely overlap, indicating a rather strong, independent strain of preaching technique which is indigenous to Black culture.

A Louisiana-born minister with a bachelor of divinity degree from a recognized Midwestern graduate school of theology was once asked what effect his theological training had had on his preaching. This minister, the son of a minister and well immersed in Black religious culture long before he went to seminary, said, "None!" This may not be strictly true in one sense, but the fact is that the man in question represents many Black preachers with strength and impact in the pulpit precisely because he kept the features he learned at home and rejected the alien notions about preaching which were promoted by his white seminary. This great sin of the seminaries is only now beginning to be corrected. Meanwhile the Black preacher must certainly be Black in style and relate in all the subtle ways he knows to his Black congregation.

VIII

The Black Sermon

In keeping with the principles of Black individuality, imagination and spontaneity, it is impossible to offer a definitive outline structure of a typical Black sermon. There is typical illustration, typical storytelling, Black language and style, and fairly typical Black climax, but the routes by which climactic utterance is arrived at are as many and varied as the preachers themselves and the various dialogues which comprise each of their sermons. We will be more concerned here, then, with such features as climax than with an exhaustive discussion of overall structure. Black preaching is as varied structurally as white preaching, although there is probably a higher percentage of sermons preached by Blacks in which the whole outline consists of the telling, at length, of a Bible story.

By the same token the percentage of typical white-type expository sermons—with text, exposition, and the inevitable trinity-of-points-plus-climax—would probably be smaller in the total experience of Black preaching. In addition, Black preaching, even when there are such points, tends not to *sound* so organized. The force of the message does not hinge so much on logical persuasion of the sort that requires the preacher to score points in an argument. Thus, when a Black preacher is most persuasive logically, he is likely to seem more to probe the depths than to argue. Symbolically, he guides his seekers rather than arguing with his opponents.

My own observations seem not to show much correlation between structure and effectiveness, or structure and response. The variations in response seem much more related to personal charisma. It would be safe to say that whites use no approach to organization of a sermon which in the hands of a given Black preacher might not be very effective with a Black congregation. It would obviously be true as well that no approach, no matter how typical of Black preaching, can guarantee effectiveness if the preacher himself does not have the charismatic gift or power to use it appropriately.

The following excerpt is from a sermon entitled "Jesus and Your Jailer," preached by the Rev. Manuel L. Scott [1] at a local church revival in Denver in the early 1960's. It has no sustained biblical narrative, nor has it many of the more common Black traits, but it was well received. Indeed, the Reverend Scott is in constant demand for city-wide Black revivals and other speaking engagements all over the country. He uses a

[1] Pastor of the Calvary Baptist Church of Los Angeles.

preaching style that is unique, but still very Black. This excerpt is an illustration of the technique of probing the depths rather than of logical persuasion. Yet it exhibits very orderly progress from point to point in its simple, easily understandable message to contemporary man.

Jesus and Your Jailer

Jesus says in Luke 4:18, "The spirit of the Lord is upon me because he anointed me to preach deliverance to the captive and to set at liberty them that are bruised."

If I were to vote the house tonight by asking the question, how many of you have ever been in jail? I feel confident that but few if any hands would go up. Although the church has not been too successful in making mature Christians, the church has been effective in keeping its members and friends within the bounds of law and order. And say what you will or may, it is an achievement to be able to say, "I've never been in jail." . . .

I have a man in my church who has eleven children. I was talking to him the other day and he said: "Rev, I've reared all of my children and I've never had to go down to talk with the judge—or get any of them out of jail." And that was something to rejoice about. But before you decide, before you make it up in your mind that you are fully free . . . before you get too happy and pat yourself on the back . . . I think you ought to bear in mind that there is another kind of jailer, prowling this land, hand cuffing and hooking folk. . . .

It is interesting to note that many of the things that would send you to hell, won't send you to the city jail. [Great response.] So don't be too delighted over the fact that no policeman has never handcuffed you! But while I talk tonight, don't look around at anybody else; go *self*-searching and see if anything has *you* imprisoned. . . . That kind of a jailer is moving through our world today. And he's impartial too. He'll lay hands on the pulpit, just like he does the pew. So you've got some *preachers* in jail —prisoners, prisoners!

Whatever you will want to quit and can't, that's your jailer. Now, you think about this: whatever exercises itself against you, whatever is not good *for* you—and it's so good *to* you that you can't let it alone—that's your jailer. . . . Whatever reduces your freedom, restricts your operation, limits your performance, whatever keeps you from doing your best—that's your jailer—that's your jailer! Whatever is greater than your will and stronger than your deepest desire—that's your jailer! It—it has you handcuffed and hooked! And I'm here to tell you that whoever you are—you'd better do something about your jailer. For, eventually, every jailer leads his victim to judgment. Some folks are just worried about the *final* judgment, but . . . life judges us *here*. . . . And some folk know what I'm talking about. There are Judgment Days right here—where a man stands face to face with his sins, and sits down to a banquet of consequences, of foolish choices, incoherent decisions. Judgment Day right here!

So—whatever has you in jail tonight, you'd better *plan* to do something about it and try to get *free* from it— 'cause it'll destroy you! Whatever it is, it's likely to let you run a long time. But Judgment Day is coming. And that thing that menaces you and makes you do what you don't want to do—that thing will mess you up! Just keep messing with it, and it will *mess* you up! . . .

Well, now let's take a look at that. In the first place, there are some people who are . . . I mean literally chained about with physical appetites and passions. The drunkard—the liquor lover who's got to have it every morning, who has to have a bottle in his bedroom and has to carry it on his job—he's in jail! The thing about liquor is that it can fool you. It makes you think you can put it down when you get ready, but try it! That's your jailer. . . .

The narcotic habit—just have to have some kind of drug, some kind of a needle, some kind of sensation— you're in jail! And I don't ever get mad at people like that; I feel sorry for them because I know they're in jail.

The Apostle Paul, I guess he was an old man, but he had learned a great lesson, and he wrote of his body, "I bring it into subjection; I don't let my appetites *enslave* me! So that, after all the work and all the labors, when I preach to others, I myself won't be a castaway!" He said, "I watch my bodily appetites so I won't be junk!"

I think I hear C. C. Harper talking about "stay off the junk pile," and don't you know this body can get you there! Just be foolish, keep on gambling, keep on using narcotics, keep on having affairs with the women, it'll get you on the *junk pile!* [Great response.] . . .

Well, I guess some of you say, "Well, Reverend, you're not talking to me because I don't drink and I don't smoke and I don't run men or chase women. I don't use narcotics nor needles. I'm not in jail to *any*body!" But there is another kind of a bondage—*bondage* of the mind, when all that you have along with you is a head full of fogy ideas. *Intellectual bondage!* And this is an awful thing because you don't see it too well! . . . Think you're right and be dead wrong. I meet men like that all the time,

and they say, "You know, all the preachers are rogues."
You aren't kidding me! All the churches are rotten?
You're in *jail!* "Nobody's going to Heaven?" You're in *jail*.
Neighbor, your mind is all wrong, and if the church is
going to win today, we've got to win the battle of ideas.
Intellectual bondage!

One of the most subtle forms of this sin is gullibility.
. . . When Jesus talked about that rich man, he called
him a *fool*. He was deceived! He *thought* that things
could make life really worth living. He *thought* that
materials could give him peace of mind. He *thought* that
somehow or other he could speak peace to his own soul!
Jesus said he was a *fool!* Well, that's the way sin got
started anyway—by Satan just deceiving somebody. . . .
Yes, if you eat of this fruit, you'll become like God, and
God knows that Adam was deceived. Because really
when he ate of the forbidden fruit, he got less like God
than before. Gullibility! You're gonna have to watch the
ideas that people are peddling around. . . . Say, while
you're young, go 'head and sow your wild oats. It's all
right, everybody did that! You're in *bondage* if you think
like that!

Well, you say, "Mind you, Rev, you're not talking 'bout
me 'cause I got all my ideas down right. . . . Ah—but
there's another kind of *bondage*. Maybe I missed you or
maybe you're gone to sleep. But you ought to wake up
now! Maybe you are in *this* class! [Great response.]

There is a bondage of the *spirit*. When you become a
slave to resentment, that's one kind of a bondage of the
spirit, you know. Just see folk you don't like to meet.
You're just resentful, and you hate to reach for their
hand. Neighbor, you're in jail! And one of the most awful
things is that some of us have to *live* with folks, sleep

with people we resent. You've got to come *out* of that jail.
. . . Isn't it awful to have to go home every evening to a
wife you don't wanna see? [Great response, dialogue.]
Resentment masters you. It shows you up in many ways
—won't let you sing well, won't let you worship well in
church. . . .

Jealousy is another kind of spiritual bondage. . . .
That's what Joseph's brethren had. . . . They said, "Well,
we got to get rid of him . . . our darling brother! . . .
contrive a machinery that will get rid of him." And
Joseph's brothers had been jealous a long time. That kind
of jealousy destroys our patience. We always try to get
rid of somebody.

Well, you have to watch what you try to destroy.
Because the very thing that you try to destroy, if you're
not very careful, it'll destroy you! Now Saul found it out
—he tried to get rid of David. But that thing killed Saul.
It killed him!

I could go on, but I must close now. I could go on and
talk about the kind of jailers that move across our world,
but I've got some good news for you. If you're in jail
tonight, Jesus is a great emancipator, yes, he is! I said he
is a great emancipator! If anybody can make you free,
Jesus can make you free. He said the spirit of the Lord is
upon me because he has anointed me to preach *deliverance* to the captives, and to set at liberty them that are
bruised.

The climax of this sermon was a Black celebration of
the freedom in Christ.

The Black sermon is a many-splendored thing, but
the example above illustrates the principle of introduction found in every good sermon, whether Black or

otherwise. Never start the message proper until you have the attention of the audience. In Black preaching it would be more accurate to state that one has to establish a kind of intimate fellowship—a rapport traditionally easily established, but in-depth.

This contrasts in degree if not in kind from white, middle-class Protestant preaching in that it has to provide the foundation for a much broader spectrum of experience and relationship. If one is to hear a preacher as the men on Mars Hill did, and it is only required that an idea be considered and people be willing to "hear thee again of this matter" (Acts 17:32), then this is one thing. If, on the other hand, it is expected that the preacher's personality and message shall be allowed to penetrate the defenses and have access to the deepest emotions of the hearer, then this is obviously a much more intense and intimate arrangement.

To arrive at this depth of involvement, every Black preacher takes a different route, and each preacher has, of course, a variety of introductions. Pastor Scott in the sermon above does it short and sweet, very economically and adroitly. When he merely mentions the possibility of jail, he has touched a theme that rushes to the deeper feelings of Black Christians. Respectable white Christians may enjoy a detachment which, because they are assured just and stable law enforcement, relegates jail to a world utterly removed. But the most pious Black man is haunted by the fear that the vagaries and the capriciousness of white "law and order" may, at any moment, make of him an undeserving sacrifice. To mention jail is to get to the heart of the matter and the man. Attention, plus emotional involvement, is guaranteed by such an introduction.

Other Black preachers tell jokes and loosen people up before the serious move to the spiritual depths of the hearer. Still others go to the pulpit and chat ad lib until they sense that the congregation is "with" the preacher, and then they launch the more serious message. Then there are those who sing or have others sing to warm up the congregation. And a few preachers count on the familiarity of the Bible to build trust and rapport. Thus they stand up preaching, and their first words are the text.

The techniques used will also vary according to previous conditioning. A beloved pastor known for twenty years needs only to walk to the pulpit to have deep rapport with most of his hearers. A revival speaker on Friday night needs far less introductory material than he did in his first message on Sunday. But the single goal underneath each of these respective approaches is to establish a situation in which the deep feelings of preacher and people may be expressed in a climate of acceptance and faith.

The spontaneity of Black preaching is nowhere more pragmatically justified than in the introduction. Since no two congregations are identical, and the mood of even a single congregation varies, every Black preacher has to size up the situation on the spot. A clever start may be planned (and no preacher in the Black idiom should stand without having some ideas for a start), but the security with which he launches forth has in the last analysis to depend on the promise that it "shall be given you in that hour" what to speak (Mark 13:11). This is true dialogue between preacher, people, and God. The Black preacher understands it and embraces the creative risk.

A final concern regarding the Black introduction might be the already obvious idea that there are really two elements in the Black introduction. They may be telescoped into one, but awareness of them is important. There is the introduction of the *speaker*—the sense in which he has to win his way inside the outer defenses and get close to the hearts of the audience. The less familiar they are with each other, the more important this aspect may become.

The second aspect is the more standard and traditional one of launching the text. The Scott transcript above omits the ad-lib comment which preceded the serious message, but it is fair to say that personal rapport of speaker with audience was well established prior to and apart from this. It would also be true that this opening comment about being in jail is an excellent means of opening both for the speaker and the text.

The Black Fathers could assume an audience range from curiosity to profound interest, so far as the Bible was concerned. The Black Bible was their chief literature and oral story source. It was precious to them. Because of this, it was necessary only to get related personally to launch the gospel dialogue. But today, Black hearers—youth especially—require some means whereby the *need* for biblical insight is established. Otherwise they could hardly care less about a text. The sermon above is only one means of achieving an effective text introduction. But it is a good one, and it illustrates the principle that modern preaching, even in Black, must lead interest *to* the text rather than assume that widespread interest in it already exists.

How a text is dealt with subsequently will vary considerably. But how it is introduced will greatly influence its effect with large numbers of youth and others. The fact that the text is there will lend authority to the message among the more traditional majority in the more typical churches of the Black masses.

The uniqueness of the Black introduction is in its relational role between speaker and audience. The uniqueness of the Black climax is similarly more related to feeling tones than to any standard set of elements. This may come as something of a surprise to some critics of the Black preacher. For these critics, every climax is stereotyped as leading to a graveyard and some tears and shouting. The Black climax, at its best, is a kind of celebration of the goodness of God and the standing of Black people in his kingdom, as these elements have been expressed in the message.

As celebration, the Black climax is not required to teach or to deal with concepts or to convey facts. Although every Black sermon should teach and enable and empower Black people, the climax consists of a kind of positive reinforcement. The hearer is permitted to relax a bit from reaching after new spiritual insight, and to lift up in confirmation and gratitude what he has already received.

In order to accomplish this, the Black preacher has shifted from objective fact to subjective testimony—

from "he said" and "it happened" to "I feel" and "I believe." While middle-class white preachers are admonished to avoid what Henry Sloan Coffin called "ecclesiastical nudism" in the pulpit, Black preachers, in climax, lay bare their souls in symbolic and contagiously free affirmation. The achievement of complete liberty in the spirit affirms the preacher's personhood in a positive, healing catharsis. But his assertion of self in the form of unlimited praise of God is a form of fulfillment in which the whole congregation participates and from which it benefits both vicariously and directly.

The Black preaching tradition has been very strong in the area of free, healing expressions and celebration. It has been very weak in making the climax relevant, either to the sermon text or to the reinforcement of Black growth and enablement. It has been much stronger in its capacity to steel and strengthen determination than in its capacity to relate to what that determination should be.

Black preachers have all too often found themselves in the predicament of serving a beef dinner and then drowning the beef in chicken gravy. Frequently the material used in climax has not been related to the substance of the message. If the gravy or climax was not mere water and flour, too often the broth has been from another bird—an imaginative flight to "get results," rather than an integral part of the message. In thus abandoning the theme for a push-button response, the Black preacher sometimes dilutes or destroys the impact of the message. The unforgettable aspect of the sermon may thus become the relatively meaningless movement or vision, while the real lesson is crowded off the stage of memory.

The critics of Black preaching may very well be correct when they suggest that the sin of irrelevant climax is born of the desire to manipulate people. But there is at least another aspect of it, particularly with men of no formal training. The search for climactic material, for most, has not been hampered by any such principles as are offered here. Nobody ever told these men that heaven or the cross was not a fit climax for all sermons. Whatever misgivings they might have had would have been traceable to their instinctive awareness that, no matter how good it is, no climax can be used too regularly. In the area of creative and relevant climax, the Black pulpit needs improvement badly, but it has within its tradition the elements of its own perfecting. Its greatest lack has been at the point of not being aware of the need for such discipline as this.

The staunch defender of the Black pulpit tradition may fear that to be so analytical about relevance will kill the climax dead. This need not be true. In fact, it may both increase effect (by means of variety) and reinforce the lesson to be taught. One of the most dramatic congregational responses I have ever been rewarded with involved what proved to be one of the most relevant climaxes I ever used. It was a Palm Sunday sermon on a comparison of the "Hosanna!" crowd and the "Crucify him!" crowd. The point was that while the vast majority of people will echo what others say, the Christian must think for himself and take a stand on what he thinks. The climax challenged people of faith to move out of the human herd and take a stand. As the climax ended and the music started, I saw a man airborne at an altitude I had never seen any shouter achieve before. How satisfying it was to know that he and all the rest were celebrating on target, and not on some extraneous point or no point at all. Here is a transcript of the last part of this climax:

> No, I don't want to be in the "Crucify Him" crowd *or* the "Hosanna" crowd. I don't want to be in *no* crowd. I don't *even* wanta be where a few people venture out and *every*body goes along. 'Cause I might wind up changin' too easy and bein' too wrong.
>
> I don't want to be in the four hundred elite. And I'll get along if they don't number me among the best dressed or the most popular. And I don't care if they don't number me in the top ten preachers.
>
> Ain't *no* number down here that I just *got* to be in—no number I really *want* to be in. But there is *one* number that I do want to be in. It's the number that John saw—the number that no man could number, coming up out of all nations and kindreds and peoples and tongues. It's the number of those that came up out of great tribulation and had washed their robes in the blood of the lamb.
>
> I don't want to be in no other number, but I want to be in *that* number. It's the number our fathers sang about when they sang "Oh, when the saints go marchin' in, oh, when the saints go marchin' in—Lord, I want to be in *that* number, when the saints go marchin' in!" [Great response.] "Oh, when they crown him Lord of all, oh,

when they crown him Lord of all—Lord, I want to be in that number when they crown him Lord of all!" [Response.] Let us pray.

A closely related example of clearly relevant climax comes from a sermon by Dr. Sandy Ray [2] on how we are "ambassadors for Christ" and thus "foreigners," sent here to represent the kingdom of God. He concludes:

> I find myself enjoying it [this world] a little too much. I find myself getting along too well here—kinda getting too well adjusted. Once in a while I want something to remind me that I'm a foreigner, and I'm a stranger, that this world is not my home.
>
> And this will not be the end, this will not be the end. Some months ago, I was rushing home to a funeral of one of my ministers, and I was going from Columbus, and in the rush I got on the wrong plane. And when I got near Washington, I was asleep and the stewardess came and shook me and said:
>
> "Fasten your seat belt—we're coming into Washington."
>
> And then she said: "This flight terminates in Washington."
>
> But I had a ticket to New York! And I got terribly distressed, and as soon as we got off in Washington, I rushed up to the counter and I said:
>
> "Look, I have a New York ticket and my flight has terminated here in Washington." And the agent said:
>
> "Oh, yes, Doctor, you go right to gate Number Two. *You have continuing reservations.*" [Great response.]

[2] Pastor of Cornerstone Baptist Church of Brooklyn, N. Y., and vice-president of the National Baptist Convention, U.S.A., Inc.

So let me tell you we must so work, and so serve, and so live, that when we come down to death, when death calls at the grave and says, "Your flight terminates here," there'll be another messenger who'll walk up and look at the ticket, and say, "*Oh, yes,* this flight does terminate, but *you have continuing reservations.*" Then, when we come to go to glory—all of us gathered from the countries where we've served, all of us called in from our ambassadorial assignments—I can *hear* the king, as he looks over us, as he looks over our records, and I don't know about you but I want him to say:

"Well done. Well done, thou good and faithful servant. You've had some rough days, and you didn't get along always too well with the foreigners, and they gave you a hard time, but you stuck it out and did a good job. Well done, well done, that's good enough!" [Great response.]

Another example of climax coming out of the body of the sermon comes from a sermon I preached on the text "Our Father." Near the end of the sermon the point was made that, when Paul says, "whereby we cry Abba, Father" (Romans 8:15), he is clearly putting God the Father on a close family basis. In English the familiar words for parents are the easy, baby words first uttered by the child. "Abba" is the obvious equivalent of "Dada" or "Daddy." The sermon goes on to say:

I remember last spring when our daughter was in a cold campus environment—in the midst of many people who didn't love her or understand her—and she felt alone. And one Sunday night she called up on the phone. Her mother accepted the charges, and she talked with her a minute or so—maybe not that long—before, with

tears that one could clearly hear in her voice, she blurted
out, "I want to talk to my Daddy!" She didn't want to ask
for any money. She didn't want permission to go somewhere. It was as if she had said, "I just wanna hear my
Daddy say something. I just gotta hear his voice!"

And when I get all upset, when my spirit is low, when
I don't know where I'm goin', and don't know what to do,
I feel just like our girl felt. "I wanna talk to my Daddy!"

When I hear his still small voice, when he moves on
the altar of my heart, when he touches that something
within, everything is all right! Let us pray.

Our Daddy—I hardly dare say it, but you are our
Daddy in heaven. . . .

The Black climax has been criticized by whites and
some Blacks as too emotional, manipulative of people
and unnecessary to the point of the sermon. The latter
challenge is met, obviously, when the climax is relevant
to the body of the sermon. It dramatizes and supports
the point.

In response to the first criticism, it must be said that
Black culture as a whole, and Black religious culture in
particular, *is* emotional. To destroy escalation of emotion in climactic utterance is by implication to do away
with the emotions of less intensity as well, and to de-
cree a flat, even, uninteresting level of involvement.
But people live by emotion. Emotions move people,
while ideas which do not generate some emotion are
powerless to change anybody's life.

In the Black climax at its best, the idea—the point
which has been made—is embraced and celebrated. It
is, as it were, burned into the consciousness of the

hearer. Embrace and celebration are emotional. And a good Black climax will appeal to the highest and noblest emotions of a man, whether Black or white. If indeed it is guilty of having manipulative power over people, it is a power capable of the liberation and uplift of Black people and all mankind. The power for good that can come from a Black climax is nowhere more forcefully illustrated than in the address of the late Dr. Martin Luther King, Jr., at the March on Washington in 1963. As he took his rhetorical flight in support of his theme of an integrated America, hundreds of thousands out of every state and race and people and tongue were swept to a crescendo of determination. "I Have a Dream" will never be forgotten, not because of its intellectual soundness, but because it moved the heart of all America, stirring the highest emotions to the noblest of intentions by means of the power of God channeled through the best of the Black climax tradition.

IX

Toward a Theology of Black Preaching

Black preaching is conditioned by the sociology, economics, government, culture—the total ethos of the Black ghetto. It is also affected by (and producing and changing) both a Black *summa theologica* and, in particular, a theology about itself. Much of this body of thought is unconscious and unformulated. However, the process of analysis and writing has begun. Professor James H. Cone's writings are especially good cases in point. It is necessary and appropriate here to consider the theology of Black preaching. This can only be a beginning, but it is very important to state this theological basis.

The Black sermon is produced in a process which has already been clearly established as deeply involving the congregation. Black folk-theology of the people has

196

always gone a step further and assumed that there was a third personal presence in the process, even the Holy Spirit. Black congregations have literally claimed the promise that "where two or three are gathered together in my name, there am I in the midst of them" (Matthew 18:20).

However stated, it has clearly been assumed that the sermon came from God. It has seldom been stated in terms of God as preacher, but the implication that God has been speaking has always been clear. In an age of secularization and emphasis on human effort, this sounds out of step and behind the times. It is necessary, therefore, to develop a theology of preaching which properly takes into account this advance in the thinking of Christendom.

This requires a collateral assumption about preparation which would appear to some as not typically Black. Men must *prepare* to preach. Many Black preachers seriously hold that specific preparation is contrary to the concept that sermons come from God. But other Black preachers (certainly those who bother to get professional training) hold that God acts only after man has done all that he can do by way of preparation. The category "man," in this case, includes the congregation. In unwitting support of the concept of man's crucial participation, many of the preachers most committed to Black culture will say, when the sermon goes hard, "Somebody isn't praying!" Thus the often unconscious assumption of Black preaching is that man brings to God his very best and asks him to take both preacher and congregation and make between them a sermon experience in which his word and will are proclaimed, with *power*.

This is not to get the least bit technical about *how* one carries out his prior effort. Be it outline, verbatim notes or just concentrated thought, prayer, and study about the text, *there must be some serious effort to give God one's best in preparation.* To do less is like asking God to do one's homework, or to go to the store and buy a loaf of bread! It should be clear in *any* theology, Black or otherwise, that God will surely not do for man what man can do for himself. This is the point of secularization in recent thought, and it must be faced. The fact that man has control now of many things for which he once had to ask in prayer must be seen to apply to every field. One of these is the field of preaching. What the unschooled and charismatic Black preacher once was literally given from on high has now to be sought in part in the modern preacher's library. *Then* may he ask of God the finishing touches. He who asks God to do the entire task hath not heard the command to subdue all things (Genesis 1:28), or to go wash in the pool of Siloam (John 9:7), or to pick up his own bed and walk (Mark 2:9 and 11). In all of these God does his part *after* man has done his.

The question immediately arises: What of the spontaneity so universally accepted as Black culture's greatest trait? The riff or improvisation on the melody, so characteristic of the Black jazz instrumentalist or vocalist, is Black spontaneity at its best. The same freedom applied to the melodic line in Black gospels or religious

Soul music is the very trademark of Black culture. One Black intellectual, who is a popular lecturer in colleges and universities, has so embraced the concept of Black spontaneity as to make each lecture an example of his own thing, created in dialogue with the class *on the spot*. Is not this collateral assumption about preparation the very antithesis of Black spontaneity?

The answer from this same model of music is most obvious. No jazzman elaborates on the theme until he has mastered the theme, the instrument and the diatonic scale. When he does his thing, creating and playing "from the bottom of his soul," he has already practiced the basics for hours. To be sure, he is creating, Black fashion, and he is in a dialogue with his audience which is comparable to the Black-preaching dialogue. But the least informed Black jazz buff can feel the difference if the artist has not done his homework. So it is with the Black preacher. His hearers want what God gives him on the spot. But they also prefer that he be properly prepared to receive God's gift, and that he should have gotten some of it in advance. God does not give by direct revelation or inspiration what man can procure of God's gifts by his own study.

These generalities about preparation require at least some more specific word with reference to the *format* in which one brings his man-made part of the sermon. The traditional phrasing of the issue is the old controversy between those who use a verbatim manuscript and those who use an outline, of whatever complexity or detail.

The first comment has to be that God can speak to a

man at his desk as well as in his pulpit. Therefore, although the end product is a dialogue with the congregation, the beginning may well be in a dialogue between the preacher and his God. This can produce both manuscripts and outlines. The old-school idea that only man speaks on the prepared paper was usually a dodge to rationalize the unlearned preachers' nonconcern with books and writing. That the very Bible itself was *written* by men inspired did not seem to trouble the antibook people. The argument against manuscripts as quenching the spirit is further riddled by the fact that in the Black pulpit there is never any such thing as a verbatim manuscript. One may read every word, but the interpretation will still be different each reading. A substantial aspect of meaning has to do with *how* it is read. This amounts to an impromptu reinterpretation each time a given manuscript is read, a creation which is still the product of the preacher, the congregation and the Holy Spirit.

The prominent preachers whose tapes I studied used manuscripts very well. But virtually all of them engaged in interludes of completely spontaneous elaborations or illustrations. On the whole, these were very plainly more effective than the passages that were read. In addition to the increased rapport with the congregation, born of the restoration of visual contact and the increased freedom and flow, there was the apparent influence of these passages as coming more from the preacher's "soul." Whether the Black manuscript preacher uses a variety of reading interpretations or lengthy, spontaneous interpolations (most use both), the fact is obvious that God uses the manuscript method in some Black preachers to His own glorification.

My own bias is a somewhat more purist approach to the spontaneity so clear in Black religious tradition. This suggests that these excellent manuscript preachers would have been still more effective if they had established their original "batting stance" in the outline tradition. (On the other hand, it's not a good idea to change the batting stance of a .350 hitter, either.) To return to the parallel of the improvisation on themes in jazz and gospel songs, the outline is comparable to the establishment of the theme. The outline helps the Black preacher to integrate the gift that God has already given in the moment of illumination in the study with what God gives directly and through the congregation when the preacher proclaims the gospel from the pulpit. In theory, at least, this outline approach seems best to provide the environment for an authentic worship-happening. In fact, God gives happenings to his Black preachers in spite of their manuscripts, and no theological construction can honestly oppose what so authentically comes from God.

Or do the best of Black sermons actually come from God? Again the single statement begets reservation. A further collateral assumption is required. Even though the Creator does speak through the medium of the Black sermon, the process is, in fact, the product of a partnership. This partnership involves not only the preparation mentioned but the goals and the entire message and impact. Whether it be styled to save and sanctify, to help and lift needy mankind, to praise God, or to hasten the very reign and kingdom of God, this means that the process of creation of the sermon is not exclusively God's.

God, who does not need anything men do, has clearly left it up to men to accept the creative partnership. If one man or all men refuse, Black theology holds that the rocks will cry out the message (Luke 19:40). But this concept of inevitable proclamation has no application to a unilateral creation of a gospel happening in our time. Rather it is directed to the end of human humility.

The creative aspect of a partnership between God and the preacher is vitally important. The hermeneutic principle clearly demands that preaching be more than fiery repetition of ancient shibboleths. No golden age of preaching to which men can look back was known at its inception to be golden. It was too fresh and disturbing. It was recognized as golden more often only in retrospect. The Black hermeneutic, at its best, will also be very strange and new. Just as the jazz riff or the gospel-song improvisation on the melody will be a brand-new creation of the moment, so must the Black sermon be fresh and immediately relevant. It is the joint enterprise of a Creator who declares, "Behold, I make all things new" (Revelation 21:5)—and a Black preacher who makes himself the instrument of innovation.

Yet newness does not imply Black uncertainty. The modern, white middle-class tendency to be tentative in the interest of intellectual honesty and integrity is a luxury ill afforded in the religion of the Black ghetto.

To be sure, there are intellectual areas where honesty demands this. The question is simply whether or not the church needs to be concerned with such. The Black worshipper is seeking the answers to visceral questions on which his very life depends. The solution of abstract problems can wait. His questions are more pragmatic and immediate. He will have to bet his life on a decision tomorrow. How shall he take his risks?

"If the trumpet give an uncertain sound" (I Corinthians 14:7–9), he will only be confused. It is to be assumed that the Black preacher has had to take the same risks. What decision did he make and on what grounds? If the grounds were adequate for so momentous a risk, they are adequate to be proclaimed with certainty and not cautiously offered alongside some casual ideas he wouldn't think of betting his life on.

There are, of course, limits to the trumpet figure. The Black preacher is not an army officer ordering men to their death. Rather he is a crucial witness declaring how men ought to *live*. If he has no certainty about where to attack the infringements on his personhood, how may his hearers begin to know? But the Black church (and it is not alone) craves and demands that the trumpet be informed and, after having done all to be informed, *certain*.

This should not be construed as meaning that open-ended questions have no place in the Black Church. It simply means that such cannot be the main vehicle of meaning of the pulpit message. It means that, when uncertain issues which are anxiety producing must be plumbed, their onus should fall on, or should be addressed to, a congregation prepared to grapple with them.

Preaching or proclamation is the functional arm of dogmatic theology. "Dogmatic" is here used, in the best sense of the word, to mean the certain presentation of today's truth in its proper setting inside the historical message and meaning of Christianity. This is not to be construed in reference to the stereotyped, hysterical, pulpit-pounding opposition against science, reason, and modern thought in general. Of this Gerhard Ebeling says:

> Yet it fails to realize its true obligation of presenting this man [modern secular intellectual], whom it regards as the enemy whom it is incapable of loving, with the testimony which would bring him the gift of certainty. Church proclamation of this sort is *de facto* propaganda against the church. . . . What is really needed is that we should find a way of witnessing to the Christian faith which is so convincingly simple and radical as to overcome problems raised by the tension between the letter and the spirit, or at least to show that they are secondary problems.[1]

The Black hermeneutic, Black preaching at its best, has done this very thing time and again. Giving the primary emphasis to the immediate needs of men and putting the intellectual questions in their secondary place, the message for *now* has been proclaimed. An excellent illustration is found in the sermon done some

[1] Ebeling, *Theology and Proclamation*, trans. by R. Gregor Smith (Philadelphia: Fortress Press, 1966), p. 19.

years ago at Bishop College [2] by Dr. Sandy F. Ray of Brooklyn, New York:

This spirit to move out into new areas grips a man here and there. Not all, but one once in a while. Remember that thrilling story of the disciples caught in the storm. It involved a man of whom I am extremely fond. Jesus appeared and saw them out in this boat, distressed. The waters were lashing, and it was terribly dark. And they wished they had waited on Him (because they had left Him behind). And someone raised the question "I wonder where He is; we should never have left Him!" "But He told us to go and He would be on later." "But now we are caught! We are caught in the grip of a storm and *we* can't manage this little boat."

And Jesus came, and the lightning flashed and somebody saw Him, and when they saw Him, they screamed, "Ghost! It's a ghost! It means that we are going to be destroyed!" And then the lightning flashed again, and Simon Peter saw Him, and they all thought, "It's a ghost."

But just in the height of the fear, Jesus said, "Stop being afraid . . . it is I." And this daring man, with reckless faith, said, "Lord, if it be Thou, suffer me to come to you walking on the water." He said, "Come on." So Simon started to leave the boat, and the other men laid a restraining hand on him and said, "Don't be stupid. . . . Be practical! . . . You've been about lakes all of your life. Haven't you had enough?" But he said, "*Jesus* told me to come." But he said, "Listen, we *all* love Him, and we all know He has great power, but that's *water*, Simon,

[2] Dallas, Texas.

and *no* man has ever walked on water!" But he said,
"That's the *Lord*." He said, "I know it's the Lord, but be
practical." But Simon said, "When the Lord calls, sometimes you lose the sense of what is practical, and right
now my faith has become reckless and daring, and I'm
going." And the records said, "He walked on the water!"

Oh, I know, I know you're going to say, "But he sank."
. . . But he walked! . . . He walked on the water! And
when he started from the boat, the laws of nature said,
"Here comes a man walking, Lord, on the water; and you
know that this is against the laws of gravitation; what
shall we do?" He said, "With faith like this, you might
suspend the natural laws, because we have to meet a
faith like this with an unusual suspension of the law. And
if he has the faith to walk . . . let him *walk!*" And the
records said, "He walked on the water." Oh, I know you
said he sank. . . . But he walked! But you say he didn't
make it. . . . But he walked! He walked long enough for
it to go in his obituary that he walked on the water. But
he was walking toward someone who could rescue him
when he sank.

Let us make man . . . make him daring . . . make him
venturesome . . . make him fearless . . . for he isn't
completed yet and his task is not completed. There is lots
yet to be done that calls for courage and strength and a
daring and reckless faith. We won't all get it . . . but we
can create a climate in which one man will walk on the
water. We won't all try something great . . . but we can
create a climate of faith in God that once in a while a
prophet can grow up. Let us make man . . . he isn't
finished yet. . . .

Thus did a Black preacher inspire a host of Black
college students to attempt the theretofore impossible.

Thus did he, in typical Black idiom, select his text for its message and not its scientific complexities. A *certain* sound was uttered about a certain issue, and the secondary matters were relegated to their rightful place.

This example also raises the issue of hope, so essential to the gospel as it must be preached to enslaved people. *All* men need both hope and certainty, but none so much as those who have so little other than hope. As the areas in which Black people can take up cudgels for themselves expand, their desperate need for hope may appear to diminish. But they will never be in the position to be numerically and physically in control, or even guaranteed justice, save by the hope that is in their faith. The most effective blows for freedom will still come from men who, like Martin Luther King, Jr., believe in so hopeful a concept as the "cosmic companionship" preached to foot-weary walkers in Montgomery.

This is an excellent example of Black preaching as help from God. It shares in the goals of God. The Presbyterian Shorter Catechism holds that the chief end of man is to glorify God and to enjoy him forever. Black preaching does not deny this. It simply holds that no sermon glorifies God which avoids his plan to uplift man. Far from a secular, humanistic requirement, this stems from the admonition that, when men see and receive the help of the preacher, they will in fact glorify God the Father which is in heaven (Matthew 5:16).

Black preaching of the Reconstruction Era could be considered a tremendous success when it simply enabled Blacks to survive massive brutality and injustice.

The church-aided organization of Black insurance companies and other businesses was virtually a stroke of genius. E. Franklin Frazier's *The Negro Church in America* describes the church's role in this crucial, Black Power-type thrust. The Black pulpit simply cannot coast on this golden age of the Black pulpit. It must give Blacks the insights and inspiration to survive *today's* social jungle, while, at the same time, arming them with the insights and inspiration to liberate themselves and eliminate oppression.

For instance, the Black preacher must keep the vivid imagery of the eagle stirring her nest (Deuteronomy 32:11), so loved in the Black Church. But, faced with the generation gap in the ghetto family, he must emphasize the awesome wisdom of the eagle, who knows when to insist that the eaglet fly on his own. He must also give a certain sound advice about emerging young adults, so that Black parents will not be threatened by the loss of the one being in regard to whom they have exercised any real power. Men will indeed glorify God in response, for parents will see their problems as they have never seen them in secular terms. Youth too will be grateful for having the rites of passage eased by seeing themselves in a new relation to the eagle's nest.

Alongside this very personal kind of preaching help, the Black preacher must also give the certain sound that helps by mobilizing the Black Church as the largest and most stable of all Black Power bases. In summoning the Sisters to boycotts which they can make more effective than anyone else can, the clear implications of Esther must be heard. They are indeed in the kingdom for such a time as this. And if they are scorned or even roughed up, what is this alongside Esther who said, "If I perish, I perish" (Esther 4:14-16)?

Texts like these are familiar and pregnant with potential for both the help of the congregation right here and now, and for the great joy that comes from the fresh expression and application of familiar Bible stories and their heroes. Emotional reinforcement is given to the point of application by means of the tremendous satisfaction and fulfillment that accompany the proclamation of the gospel in Black spiritual power.

The sermon which celebrates without giving help is an opiate. The sermon which tries to help without celebration is, at least in the Black Church, ineffective. The climax is a necessity. But this is not to canonize a cultural habit. Rather, it is to theologize concerning this aspect of Black preaching.

Highly liturgical churches refer to their priests as "celebrating" the Mass. (The actual history of this term would be interesting indeed.) It is not necessary to legitimize joy and celebration in worship. The fruit of the spirit is joy (Galatians 5:22). The baby of Pentecostal joy must not be thrown out with the bath water of public glossolalia, or speaking in tongues. In modern times, the joy of Black worship has been self-validating to all save the most closed-minded. The "trip" sought by the drug culture has been recognized by more than one hippie as akin to the joy of Black worship.

What is this mass expression theologically? To say that Black worship succeeds in developing joy is not to say that it is automatically right. Just as the joy of the *spiritus sanctus* (Holy Spirit) was confused with the joy of *spiritus frumenti* (alcohol) in the eyes of the unbelieving in Acts 2, so is it possible to confuse spiriis in the church today.

At its best, however, Black worship must have joy in its highest and purest form. At his best, the Black preacher must be not only a teacher and mobilizer, a father figure and an enabler, but also a celebrant. He must have a little of the joy *himself*. It must be clear that he is filled by the same joy he declares to his congregation. If indeed the preacher has not tasted and seen that it is good, he has nothing, really, to say. The goodness of God must not be a distant theory; it must be a present fact, which to experience is to celebrate. The same can be said of the goodness of the life which God gives.

To sense the presence and total acceptance of God, especially when one lives in an unaccepting, hostile world, is to know joy unspeakable. If this is literally true, how may one hold his peace? Even if one has white-oriented cultural inhibitions, if he has an open mind, how can he fail to participate in the joy of his fellow celebrants, be they laity or clergy? In their pilgrimage through the torture chamber of three hundred and fifty years of oppression, this celebration of the goodness of God and his acceptance of man has been the strongest nourishment available to Black people. It has reinforced and celebrated identity scorned everywhere else. Indeed, the Black Church itself has been made to think of its emotional freedom as a sign of primitiveness. Witness the fact that Blacks sober up

and get "dignified" in most churches when they have
white company. Fortunately, this kind of overt self-
rejection has never prevailed sufficiently to destroy the
catharsis and healing of the shouting, celebrating Black
Church. If Blacks, who have had the best reasons for
self-destruction, have traditionally left suicide to the
white American, the Black preacher had better not stop
celebrating now! And those who do not know how to
celebrate had better learn the art. In Black-worship
celebration, selfhood is validated, identity is reinforced, and the courage-to-be is renewed in the accepting, healing, uplifting presence of God. Since little else
in the world can accomplish this for Blacks, there
seems to be a valid argument for holding on to so vital
a tradition.

To assert so much about the Black preacher's role in
a day of diminishing faith is to suggest a Black tradition about the call of the minister which is not shared
in the standard white church. While they insist, in
white middle-class religion, on the conversational tone
in preaching, they also insist on the preacher blending
into the background of congregational lay conversers.
Black preachers know better. If Jeremiah (Jeremiah
1:5) could be called before birth, so can they. And if
Jeremiah's call could sustain him through unbelievable
trials and rebuffs, it can for Black preachers also. And it
has. In a day when the Black preacher has to play
many roles and be a multitude of things to *all* men, and
especially to Black men, it would be easier to escape
the call for a less taxing responsibility were it not for
the "fire shut up in my bones" (Jeremiah 20:9). The

priesthood of all believers is a fact, but the burden of the priesthood still falls heavily on the Black preacher. Today's educated young Blacks would probably avoid it in larger numbers were it not for the fact that "woe is unto me if I preach not the gospel!" (I Corinthians 9:16) is still a powerful stimulus in the Black tradition.

These, in brief, are some of the theological assumptions which underlie Black preaching. To engage in the business of Black preaching without such undergirding is either to be wanting in sincerity or to labor without support. In either case, it is to attempt the impossible, and fail. Black preachers cannot afford merely to *seem* Black. If they have not the Black theological frame of reference, then they ought to preach from the frame of reference which they do have.

X

The Black Pulpit
of Tomorrow

One of the likeliest criticisms to be leveled at this book is that it seeks to define and propagate a pulpit tradition that is already obsolete and irrelevant. To put it kindly, there are many thoughtful Black people who think Black preaching has outlived what may have been a great usefulness at one time. Many others would put it in much more critical terms. Anticlericalism in the Black community is increasing. Stereotypes and caricatures of Black preachers abound. What good reason, they ask, can be given for not letting or even helping the preaching tradition and the influence of the Black preacher die?

The answer, of course, is that the best of the Black preaching tradition considered here is not and never has been like the popular stereotype. That there are some preachers who fit the stereotype cannot be denied, but the limits of the stereotype do not require argument. The purpose of this book has been to analyze the preaching genius of the best of Black pulpiteers so that the tradition will at least be given the understanding and appreciation which it deserves, and so that its strength and influence will continue and increase. Whether the models studied here have been in a minority or a majority in the Black Church pulpit, the Black community needs more like them. Whether they will now dominate the scene as they did in the Reconstruction Era, or simply aid and discipline a much broader Black Revolution, there is not yet a better means of getting the Brothers together. The Black pulpit is a power base of great importance to all Black men.

However, even after one has granted the personal impact for good and the social relevance of the giants of the Black pulpit, it is true that some shifts and improvements must be made. The glories of the past, no matter how great, will not suffice for the future in this or any age. The Black pulpit of the future must develop along a variety of new lines, in keeping with the dynamic changes everywhere apparent.

The most ardent Black churchman must concede that the best of Black preaching and worship has tended to be an end in itself. It might be better to say that its impact has tended to heal *individuals*—to celebrate and support Black identity and support the church—but not to involve either folk or institution adequately in some scheme for liberation. At times it would seem that the music and message were so good that none dared break the spell with practical considerations of campaigns and strategy for this-world liberations. The people felt *too* healed and whole. This could be dangerous, it might be argued, to a proper perspective of present disabilities and present needs.

To assess this danger one has to establish a comprehensive model of ministry. The pulpit and public worship must be only a part of the whole impact of the church. Perhaps they have loomed too large in the total life of the Black Church, but there has been no low conspiracy to bring such a situation about. The present pattern evolved from a natural habit of following the line of least resistance—of not pressing the ghetto-handicapped Brother beyond his narrow range of capacities. The least aggressive Brother was capable of taking part in worship. The most obvious need is for the ministry to make a massive assault on the practical limitations of the Black laity, so that they are enabled to take part in a broad range of practical efforts on their own behalf. An essential part of this enablement is achieved in the healing of identity and imparting of purpose possible in worship, but the practical skills required of the laity demand substantial additions to typical Black Church strategy and program.

After the enablement-of-laity phase, the Black laity and the Black Church must relate to and be the catalyst for community-wide Black operational unity. The church institution may not be as prominent in the new Black galaxy as once it was, but its presence and ministry may still serve as the saving salt and lifting leaven it was and is called to be. It must still be the church, and never be subservient to any save the Lord of the universe, but the ministry of the Black Church must increase dramatically in the areas of enablement and involvement in the race-wide struggle that is the Black Revolution.

The place of pulpit and public worship in these aspects of the model is not easily defined. On the one hand, "preachin' and prayin' and singin'" has kept us together and helped us survive. It is an effective element, and one ought not to tamper with success. To dominate worship with Black mobilization and strategy would make it into a secular rally and kill it dead. On the other hand, public worship is the only time the Brethren are sure to gather. Work schedules and long-standing loyalties conspire to make it so. To attempt to separate educational enablement and practical involvement in Black liberation from worship would be to take them out of the mainstream and sentence them to death. Clearly a model is needed which somehow preserves the spiritual transport of Black worship and yet guarantees the growth and involvement of the salient elements of the church's ministry. Anything less evades reality.

The marriage of ecstasy and involvement is so old one wonders why it dare be said that a new model is needed. In the exodus from Egypt, Moses ordered strict observance of the people's religious rites. It was, after all, a liberation ordered and initiated by God, to be entered into with tactical dexterity and holy awe. The gathering of the Hebrews into assemblies for preparation did not degenerate into sloganistic rallies. The entire movement of these human servants of the most high God was in response to his will and action. On the one hand, Moses insisted, with economic realism, that the children of Israel keep their flocks. This was both for purposes of religious sacrifice and, obviously, for food. On the other hand he ordered the preparation of unleavened bread as a symbol of spiritual depth and discipline.

When Dr. Martin Luther King, Jr., walked across the forbidden park in Birmingham, or up the road from Selma, it was after such holy observances as a Black sermon and a warm, inspiring Soul service. The effectiveness of the combination of social action and relevance with deep awareness of the presence and will of God was attested to by many from outside Black culture, who found themselves caught up in and blessed by the experience.

Still acting within the framework of Dr. King's Southern Christian Leadership Conference, one of the most relevant ministries of today follows the same pattern. Dr. Jesse Jackson preaches and the people sing and pray, and then they launch a campaign that packs a wallop in the placement of Blacks in the Chicago job market. The name of this ministry is Operation Breadbasket. It is a very literal illustration of the marriage between ecstasy and involvement. It was born of meetings in the churches and with the full cooperation of Black clergy. It moved from the sanctuaries only when it had exceeded their physical capacities. The pastors still are in the vanguard, although the movement has long since taken on an identity of its own. The fact remains that the Black Church holds the all-time record for mobilization of Blacks in behalf of their liberation, here and in the world to come. Black preaching and Soul worship have accomplished what nothing else has ever approached.

Even with such a model of relevance in Black preaching, the theme of dynamic change must be sounded. Black culture and communication within the Black-ghetto churches are heavily under the influence of the Southern rural setting in which, until very recently, most Blacks had been born and reared. Such city-oriented culture and communications systems as Blacks have developed have largely been related to the street culture and not the church life. The Black churches have been rightly praised as the most effective conserver of Black culture. But changing scenes and situations demand a changed set of images and symbols. No longer can a preacher mention the cotton patch and the mule, and then reach his ex-cotton-picker audience so effectively that his task is done. In the Black Church pew in the Black ghetto are many who have never so much as seen a patch of cotton. What they have heard about cotton or tobacco has given them no romantic feelings or down-home nostalgia about its cultivation and harvesting. Preaching must still use the rural figures dear to parents of these city-bound Blacks, but it must also use parables and illustrations out of their own urban life.

The fact that the Bible comes from a primarily agrarian culture renders today's task somewhat harder, but it does not render it impossible. For instance, there are three parables from Jesus on the subject of something lost: the Lost Coin, the Lost Boy (the Prodigal Son), and the Lost Sheep. Of these, the coin story is quite relevant to the urban experience, and the chances are that the son in the story of the prodigal got lost in the bright lights, excitement and freedom of a big city. The lost-sheep image has little relevance to the city experience, and yet a little adaptation might give it real impact, moving the action from the wilderness where the small sheep was lost to the asphalt jungle, where small children get lost every day and parents leave the rest of the family to hunt for them.

Imaginative adaptation with the city flavor is a must if the current and future generations of young Blacks are to be reached by the gospel. There is a great hunger for such imagery, and Black people respond to Black-preaching relevance of this sort, regardless of age. The impressive numbers drawn to attend Chicago's Operation Breadbasket hear this kind of relevance, as exemplified by the sample of Dr. Jesse Jackson's Bible interpretation already given.[1] Here, it may be remembered, the Hebrew children who were put into palace training for government service were accurately portrayed as having entered the downtown power structure without surrendering either their loyalty to their God or their loyalty to their race.

My own rendition of the parable of the Unmerciful Servant includes such obvious city-culture details as an auditor and a two-dollar ticket on a race horse. The

[1] See Chapter V, "The Black Bible."

contrast may perhaps be better seen in a direct comparison of my rendition of putting the hand to the plow
and not looking back [2] (a rural figure), with my treatment of a track meet (Hebrews 12:1–2) and the use of
such track rules as that against looking back while you
run, well known to city boys (Philippians 3:13–14).
This rule, it will be seen, has been moved from the
plow, where looking back makes you plow a crooked
furrow, to the track meet, where looking back can get
you hurt. The technique here is to shift the appeal from
the primarily middle aged and older group to the
youth, and the growing numbers of adult Blacks who
have come to love track meets because they are dominated by Blacks. Yet the track-meet figure is as biblical
and as loaded with deep religious significance as the
earlier figure of the plow and the mule.

The transcript of the sermon using the track-meet
figure, for purposes of the comparison mentioned
above, is given here:

> The writer of Hebrews said this life is like a race, and
> you got to run with patience. You gotta lay aside all of
> the weight, all of the sin, and strip down to a gym suit;
> and then you got to run, looking ahead to Jesus who ran
> way ahead of you. You just got to look up there. Paul
> said you got to press. He's talking about a race too. He
> said you got to press for the mark—you got to press for
> the end of this race, for the mark of the prize of the high
> calling of God in Christ Jesus. Can't run any other
> way. . . .

[2] See Chapter V, "The Black Bible," presenting a Black-experience
parallel to Luke 9:62.

One day I said to a friend of mine who is a track star at the University of Redlands, "Elliott, tell me what Paul's talkin' 'bout. You're a track man. Tell me, what happens if you turn your head?" Elliott said, "Well, Rev, I tell you, last weekend U.C.L.A. had a man who was about to win a race. He had about four or five yards' lead." He said the boy's name was some well-known name. Then he said, "The boy was doing good, but all of a sudden he got to worryin' 'bout what was behind him." And he said he turned to look to see what was going on, and in that split second he lost just enough steam that all the lead he had was lost, and somebody nipped him at the tape.

He said you can't look back because you lose speed when you look back. You got to keep lookin' ahead. And he told me somethin' else: "One time I was runnin' and I didn't look ahead where I was supposed to, and I got my feet all tangled up, and I like to broke my neck. I got clear off the track 'cause I was lookin' the wrong way."

This is what Paul is talkin' 'bout. Paul must have been very much interested in what we would call Olympic competition. And Paul, when he talks about pressing for the mark of the prize of the high calling of God in Christ Jesus, is saying, "You gotta keep lookin' *ahead*. There ain't no way in the world you can win this race with your head turned around backward." About the best you can do is slow down, and the worst that could happen is that you would fall and break your neck.

Another shift in the balance of images and symbols is required between positive and negative. Black preaching has a holdover of white Puritanical influence, but it also has its own home-grown "no-no" tendencies from the frugalities of the predominantly farm culture in which Blacks lived. On the poverty-stricken Southern farm, Black and white alike were forced to postpone the simplest pleasures most of the time. When a good crop did come in, the habit was too entrenched to be changed for that brief, if happy, season. They had developed a very functional emphasis on self-denial. To Black youth living in a modern urban society whose affluence is paraded before them daily on television, a sermon on self-denial would seem to come from the Stone Age. When applied to material things, it would appear to them to be a tool of the white majority designed to keep Blacks happy with a lesser share of America's blessings. In such a setting as this Blacks must be made to know that there is biblical sanction for their fullest participation in the blessings of American productivity.

One need not preach an overemphasis on material things to be able to preach about positive living and profound joy. The following transcript of a sermon on abundant living [3] is an illustration of positive emphasis in the Black idiom. It was apparently a Christmas sermon preached sometime in the middle 1960's.

Jesus said, "I am come that they might have life and that they might have it more abundantly." Despite the sour stereotype of religion, despite the long face that so many people have hung like a crepe on the door of the church, the real message of this Christmas Day and of the whole of the life of Christ is summed up in the words

[3] The text was from John 10:10.

of the carol "Joy to the World." Not sourness, not long-facedness, not meanness, but *joy* to all the world! Christianity is happiness on *this* earth as well as unlimited joy after that in heaven.

In Matthew 9:15 we read where Jesus was asked about the fact that he was not a typical religious enthusiast. They were critical of his joviality, and they questioned him—you remember, they said, "John's disciples fasted and so forth and so on, and you sit up here and eat good food and have a *good* time." And Jesus answered them and said, "Can the children of the bridechamber mourn as long as the bridegroom is with them?" And this was, to a far greater extent than we usually realize, the tone and tenor of our wonderful Lord. He was a *joyous* Lord, and he came to bring *us* joy in the spirit and to help us "live it up."

Yes, there's time to mourn; there's time to fast; there's time to sleep, and time to eat. There's time to do all these things. But in the presence of God you celebrate! And perhaps our Black churches, more than any other churches in the world, have caught the spirit and come to sense how this is so. It's "Joy to the World!" and if you haven't got any joy, you haven't got any of Jesus in the first place.

Somebody is bound to say, "But didn't Jesus say in a much much better known passage than the one you quoted that a man was supposed to *deny* himself and take up his cross and follow him?" [Matthew 16:24; Mark 8:34; Luke 9:23] And of *course* he said it, but what he was saying was, "Yes, deny the eager ego, and affirm the *Imago Dei*. Deny your selfishness and affirm the spirit of God that is at work in you. For the spirit of God is joy!" The fruits of the spirit are first of all *joy*.

The abundant life referred to above has, according to many stereotyped criticisms of the Black ministry, been taken all too seriously. This not only raises the problem of balance between unselfishness or self-denial and the joyously abundant life. For the purposes of this work it raises the issue of the inevitable connection between a preacher's life style and his message, the possible conflict of images between the suffering servant and the abundant liver. How one lives speaks louder than what he says, and if his profession is to "say" or preach, the comparison between words and living witness is intensified. If one could be freed completely from the nagging of narrow, puritanical critics, he would still be haunted by the spirit of his own best preaching efforts. In Black-culture churches the Black Baptists are far more permissive about the petty moralities than their counterpart white Baptists, but the feeling of closeness already referred to many times makes every action of the pastor-preacher a family concern. To this intimacy between a pastor and his church must be added a new factor—the critical astuteness of today's generation of Black youth. With all this scrutiny, both loving and critical, the Black preacher of tomorrow is under extreme obligation to practice what he preaches.

And the issue is not the old-fashioned concern for the petty taboos which shaped the code of behavior for the pastor and his people. While a cigarette can in fact be deadly, smoking it is no longer a major issue of intelligent concern in the church. What is at issue is the overall scale of values. If the minister is, in the sight of sincere people of faith, entirely too "comfortable," he can never tell people to seek first the kingdom of God with conviction. His preaching has already been done when he filled his closet with extravagantly costly suits and shoes. The day may have been when this was required or at least permitted for purposes of the "successful" image. But that day is fast passing if not indeed past. The value system of the Black preacher must project, now, the *servant* image. The competent servant must be reasonably provided for, but if he insists on extremes and has a life style associated with great wealth, then the youth of the new Black masses will be turned off by the church and the pulpit. For them, one's scale of values and commitments speaks first and, often, last.

This means, also, that the preacher's risk taking is read. When the chips are down and the welfare of the Black man is at stake, the preacher who is security conscious and avoids the fray has already preached all the sermon he will be able to preach to many Black youth. Their awareness is significantly more acute than that of their grandparents. The stance of the preacher in the struggle may not easily win them, but it can easily lose them. If the preacher avoids the exposed positions or gives any evidence of selling out, his call to serve Black youth is already rescinded. No art or genius in the pulpit can thereafter be significant.

On the other hand, a pastor may have a membership which favors escape. They may be "out of it" and insisting that their preacher be likewise. It is here that the really sincere Black preacher must lean on his Lord and exercise the gifts that have made the Black pulpit, at its best, so relevant. The congregation that is fed and moved by the gospel is far more likely to leave its pastor free, even if he has to have patience with them while they grow to proper involvement.

Someone has said that, whatever the risk, the preacher must be a beacon in his community and not a rainless cloud. The involvement, risk taking, and leadership of the Black preacher have still the capacity to lead and inspire. The tradition is not dead, and men of courage, skill, and integrity may yet lift it to higher heights.

One of the greatest problems of integrity, however, comes not at the point of community involvement, but in the pulpit itself. No longer does the Black parson have time to meditate on the message. The quiet and deep reflection which built the best tradition of the Black Fathers is scarce these days. Long hours at the plow were far better for reflection than today's hurry and scurry. Jesus went about doing good. But today's Black pastor has to do so much going about that he, along with white pastors, sometimes doesn't get as much good done as he should, especially in pulpit preparation.

A widespread solution, unheard of in the years of earliest and greatest need, is the "canned" commercial sermon. These sermons are designed for the man who has to say something rather than for the man who has something to say. These printed counterfeits are almost always neither Black nor relevant. The preacher who Blackens them with his skillful, spontaneous adaptation and delivery will only advance the subtle sins they almost always contain.

The real answer is a fresh start, from Black need to the Black Bible to the Black experience. If a Black pastor has need of training in order to break the canned-sermon habit—a habit worse than drugs—let it never be said that any theological school was so rigid as to refuse to give him all-out assistance to this end. The Black Church and pulpit must, at whatever cost, have both personal integrity and Black relevance. There can be no truly independent and relevant pulpit which passes on to the congregation the printed signals of any man other than the pastor.

A final consideration for the future must involve further pursuit of an issue raised earlier on what is Black. In the process of defining the Black Fathers and the Black orientation of the earliest Black Church tradition dealt with here, the impression is at least possible that the Black-culture preaching here defined is only for *certain* Blacks. It is also within the realm of possibility, despite the statement about disappearing distinctions among the Black churches, that one might be led to decide that the really Black preacher cannot reach, nor would he desire to reach, that host of Blacks who speak only standard or nearly standard English. This kind of an issue requires consideration also because I have so clearly emphasized the need for better communication with the Black masses.

In the first place, the influence of white middle-class culture is so pervasive that no book need be devoted to the description of the use of that culture among and between Blacks fluent in it already. It would help to explore the unique aspects of the middle-class Black Church's worship and needs, but the more crucial problem of our time is that Black men whose training is oriented toward the needs of the white middle class have trouble reaching the Black proletariat. Nevertheless, nothing I have said should be construed to mean that I am proposing to isolate the professionally trained Black clergyman from the very group out of which he may have come, or to keep others from outside the Black middle class from serving them after professional preparation.

Whatever class the trained Black preacher of the future may come from, he must be able and equipped to reach any culture through which the Black Church finds expression. He must have what one preacher called four speeds forward and one reverse, so as to be able to fit any type of Black Church in which he may have the honor and opportunity to serve, and to diminish the gaps between the various segments of the Black community. By being multicultural, he must be all things to all segments, not only that he might save them but also that he might draw them together.

Many who are totally committed to Black liberation are, on principle, opposed to Black English. To wait until they grant its legitimacy before working for unity would be to wait entirely too long. That is to say nothing of how defeating it would be to wait until they agree to use the Black idiom. Whatever the implications about identity that may be involved here, the fact is that the Black struggle cannot bear the disunity that would issue from a judgmental stance on this score. The Brothers cannot afford to engage in a Blacker-than-thou contest.

Because Blacks simply must be together, the churches at the ends of the spectrum of Black religious culture must be open to the possibility of Blackeniza-tion, on the one hand, and to elements of relevant uplift involving what appears to be standardization on the other. Otherwise, in addition to the accusation of social distance and racial disunity, the Black churches of some areas will have the dubious distinction of having to move out of their neighborhoods because of cultural contrasts with their new Black neighbors.

The Black preacher in America is called to preach to *all* Blacks. If he can do so effectively, he will automati-cally be able to preach effectively to all kinds and conditions of men of *every* race. To learn well the tradition of the Black Fathers and interpret it in ways relevant to contemporary Black need will add immeas-urably to the strength of the whole of the Christian church and not just the Black Church. It will at least add its own distinctiveness to the Aryan and Teutonic influences mentioned earlier to the greater glory of the God who is no respecter of persons, and to the saving enrichment of the ministries of all of the churches of whatever tradition.

XI

The Gospel—in Black and White

Modern study of the Bible is very frequently assisted by two or more versions printed side by side for comparison. Perhaps a scheme such as this will serve to help to illustrate what a sermon in Blackese is like by contrast with a sermon in whitese.

Before engaging in the "translation," certain limits to the process must be noted. One is that to start with a white sermon is to start in all probability with a non-Black sermon goal. Complex goals cannot be translated in the same sense that a single simple goal can be translated and implemented in two cultures, and there are limits even to this. Another limitation is that, for these purposes at least, the translation must become a fairly plausible Black sermon. This would eliminate rather than translate some quotes, ideas, and illustrations, while possibly adding others. Yet another limitation is the fact that Black sermons, as has been noted previously, lose tremendously when put into print. Perhaps more accurately, an authentic Black sermon comes into being only in spoken dialogue. Even so, the contrast I am about to attempt should yield insight and justify the effort. It may also provide a kind of humor, helping readers of either culture to see themselves and their culture less seriously and yet more profoundly.

The sermon chosen was preached by Dr. Ernest T. Campbell, minister in the Riverside Church in the city of New York.[1] Its theme and goal have to do with clarity of the very sort the translation is intended to promote. And yet the Black goal has to be different. When Dr. Campbell instructs middle-class people and religious professionals to avoid complicated intellectual language about Christian faith, the Black pastor has to admonish the Black pillars of the church to use popular doctrinal terms out of the nineteenth century only if they clearly translate them into the conversational vocabulary of the "sinner." He cannot ask them to surrender the God-talk so dear to them.

However, when Dr. Campbell declares the half that is a "mystery" and cannot be expressed in words, he is in territory long occupied by Blacks. If it could be proved that such proclamation had no other modern relevance—and this is highly improbable—this aspect of the message in Black would be justified by the emphasis and approval it gives to the Black religious experience and the support it gives to Black identity.

[1] January 26, 1969.

The Craving for Clarity
by
Dr. Ernest T. Campbell

"If thou be the Christ, tell us plainly." (John 10:24b)

1. Some wag in a moment of pique declared that every profession was a conspiracy against the laymen. He went on to elaborate by suggesting that lawyers keep us dependent on their services by embalming the law in legalese—a mix of ancient English and encrusted Latin. That doctors keep us in our place by using long and technical words to describe our ailments. That scientists keep the little man at bay by resorting to symbols and language that only the initiate can understand. And, what is important for our purposes, the theologian and ministers in particular, and the church in general, keep themselves in business by deliberately confounding the simple verities of religion: faith, hope and love.

1. *Some rascal has said that the big-shot professionals have ganged up on ordinary folks. He seems to think that lawyers do all their work in big words so we won't know what they're talkin' 'bout. That Latin is to keep you needin' and payin'. And don't even mention the doctor. When he gets through explainin' what's wrong with you, just say, "Uh-huh," and write the check. 'Cause he could try all day to tell you, and in some of these cases you still wouldn't know what he was talkin' 'bout.*

But now did it ever dawn on you that preachers and deacons and missionary Sisters and Sunday-school

*teachers use words that sinners and young Christians
listen to the same way you listen to a doctor? They
don't know no more about what you talkin' 'bout than
you know what the doctor is talkin' 'bout.*

2. This last charge is not unlike the charge that was
leveled at Jesus that day in the temple. It was winter
and he and his followers sought the shelter of Solomon's porch. The Feast of Dedication was being celebrated. Suddenly Jesus found himself hemmed in by
angry Jews who turned upon him and said, "How long
will you keep us in suspense? If you are the Christ, tell
us plainly." This word "plainly" is one of John's favorite
words; he uses it some nine times in his gospel. It
means "without the obscurity of a parable," "openly
and publicly." "If you are the Christ, tell us plainly."

2. *This is an old problem. The church has always
had a language of its own. In our scripture lesson, the
people even accused Jesus of not bein' too plain. It was
winter time, and Jesus and 'em was at the temple in
Jerusalem. And I guess it was cold, so they was standin'
out of the wind on Solomon's Porch. And it was during
the Feast of Dedication. And I guess Jesus was talkin'
and his followers was listenin' very close.*

*So some Jews that wasn't followers saw it and
ganged around and tried to figure out why he was so
powerful. They said somethin' like "Who you? Doin' all
this speakin' and teachin' and tellin' people what to do!
How long are you goin' to keep us wonderin'? Don't use
all this power on people and we don't know from what
you say whose hands we are in. If you are the Christ,
just come on out and say it, plainly."*

3. This question might have been raised to bait Jesus, to have him declare himself categorically so that an arrest could be made. On the other hand, the request might have been born out of a deep desire to understand who he was. Let us be generous and concede the second motive.

3. *Now we really don't know what they were up to. They coulda been tryin' to get him to say somethin' wrong so they could put him in jail. But on the other hand, they mighta really wanted to know. Let's just say that's what it was.*

4. But Jesus would not oblige! The lack of communication implied in their question did not lie in his inability to tell but in their inability to hear. It is true that nowhere in his earthly ministry did he say to these people flatly, "I am the Christ." He didn't wish to do this, in part because it might have led to crucifixion prematurely, and in part because the term "Christ" or "Messiah" had been given so many different meanings that he might have been misunderstood. We cannot really answer another man's *question* until we understand the other man's *meaning* of that question.

4. *But Jesus didn't answer that question. They didn't know who he was, but it wasn't 'cause he hadn't told 'em and showed 'em too. Like he said in the next verse, "I told ya, and ya didn't believe it." Now, of course, he never did say, "I am the Christ," just in those words. If he had, they mighta crucified him much sooner. And then again, this word "Christ" or "Messiah" had so many meanings he still might have been misunderstood. You remember Judas joined Jesus thinkin' he*

*meant one thing when he meant somethin' else. That's
why he betrayed him. So Jesus didn't answer a quick
yes or no, because everybody there could have taken it
to mean somethin' different.*

5. On the other hand, Jesus had referred to himself
as the bread of life, the water of life, the son of man,
the good shepherd, the light of the world. He had done
many mighty works. He had forgiven sin. "If Thou art
the Christ, tell us plainly." Apparently he had been
plain enough for James and John and Peter and Andrew, plain enough for Mary of Magdala, the Demo-
niac of Gadara, Zacchaeus, for Mary and Martha of
Bethany and a host of others.

5. *But Jesus had said who he was in simpler words:
"I am the bread of life." "I am the water of life." He
used titles like "Son of Man," "Good Shepherd," and
"Light of the World." And, like he said, he had done
some very mighty works, like forgive sin and heal people. Talkin' 'bout "If thou be the Christ, tell us plainly!"
Apparently it was plain enough to James and John—
Peter and Andrew—Mary Magdalene—little short Zacchaeus—Mary and Martha, and a whole bunch more!*

6. Communication is not achieved by clarity alone.
The question of one's affinity for truth is also in the
picture. We come at truth with a mind set, either to
receive or to reject. Jesus spoke in parables so that
those who wished to hear might hear, and those who
had no disposition to hear could not. Notice these
words from the eighth chapter of St. Luke: "To you it
has been given," said Jesus to the disciples, "to know
the secrets of the kingdom of God; but for others they

are in parables, so that seeing they may not see, and hearing they may not understand" (Luke 8:10).

6. *You see, you don't get to understand people just by them speakin' plain. You also got to be really* lookin' *for truth. There never was a plainer teacher than Jesus. But the very parables that helped disciples confused others. In the next couple of verses Jesus explained it: "You don't understand me, you don't believe me 'cause you ain't one of my sheep. They hear my voice!"*

7. We must meet truth partway. We must come to it with readiness, expectation and imagination, and the willingness to participate in it. We suffer in our society from a lack of imagination. Auden has traced the blame for this to the advent of television. In the old days of radio one had to meet the program partway. I had my mental image of what Amos and Andy looked like and you had yours. I had my picture of the Lone Ranger and you had yours. We met the program partway. But with television, it is all there before us, and the imagination goes to sleep. We are not induced, except on rare occasions, to participate. Jesus in effect is saying that the truth about who I am sounded but you have not heard. One thinks of a tourist in the Metropolitan Museum standing before a masterpiece and saying, "I don't see anything in that." Another tourist whispers in reply, "Don't you wish you could?" "If you are the Christ, tell us plainly." The answer is clear: "When you are ready to hear, you will."

7. *Truth ain't goin' to run you down and hit you in the head and jump in. You gotta be ready for it. You gotta welcome it and go out and meet it. Hebrews says*

that, if you are lookin' for God, you got to first believe that he is, and that he will reward them that diligently seek him. Jesus says, "I done told ya who I am, but you can't hear it. When you get ready to hear, when you use your ears to hear, you'll get the message."

8. This same demand of clarity is made on the church, and not without justification. "If he is the Christ, tell us plainly. Our times are out of joint. We are hungry for a word. If he is the Christ, tell us plainly." It is in order that the church repent for having failed to declare the message of Jesus Christ with greater clarity. We have developed a jargon that speaks to those on the inside but says precious little to the man outside.

8. *Now Jesus said it very plainly. But we church people don't always do it that way. The world is saying to us, "If he is the Christ, tell us plainly." But we talk to each other about "sinners" and "grace" and "blood" and "Holy Ghost" and "Saved" and "Sanctified." And the man in the world doesn't know what we mean.*

9. Did you ever sit down in the wee hours of Christmas Eve to assemble a toy that you had purchased for one of the children? A note on the carton declares that a child could put it together in five minutes. You come upon a sleazy diagram that looks as though it were the last copy coughed up by a tired A. B. Dick machine at the end of a long run. "Tell us plainly," you whisper hopefully. And the instructions come: "Take crossbar A and fasten to upright C, keeping the flanged edge to the lower center. Tighten Ferguson bolt, making sure lock washer is facing bar B. Insert bracing rod into opening C, making sure corner braces are at 90° angles

to tube D. Snap end rods in place by pressing with thumb at point A-2. Attach wheels as marked."

10. The world turns to the church and says, "If he is the Christ, tell us plainly." Karl Barth answers with eleven thick volumes of *Church Dogmatics*. Tillich answers with three closely reasoned volumes of theology. Bultmann answers with two volumes of *New Testament Theology* and a complicated work on demythologizing. "Tell us plainly." They ask for bread and we give them a stone, they ask for fish and we give them a scorpion.

11. Perhaps most of the blame lies with us who are ministers at the local level, for it is part of our job to understand what the theologians are saying, break their language down, and share it with our people. Unfortunately, we pastors are frequently as obtuse as the theologians. I remember the feeling of letdown that overtook me when the father of the bride slipped me a book following his daughter's wedding. It was entitled *Write Clearly, Speak Effectively*. How did he know? He had never heard me preach!

12. T. S. Eliot comments on this precarious business of word selection when he writes in "Burnt Norton," "Words strain, crack and sometimes break, under the burden, under the tension, slip, slide, perish, decay with imprecision, will not stay in place, will not stay still."

13. Our speech must be clarified and also our understanding of the meaning of what we say. It is the theologian's task to clarify the church's talk about God. The linguistic analyst in turn helps the theologian clar-

ify his talk about God by asking repeatedly, "What do you mean by that?" And all of this is to the good, for density is not a virtue even when practiced by Christians. "If he is the Christ, tell us plainly."

9–13. *It's like some guy walks up to you talkin' 'bout "Donde esta la iglesia?" You don't know what he's askin', let alone the answer. You speak English and he speaks Spanish. If he is the Christ, the boss, the one who can help me, tell me in my mother tongue. If I'm a Galilean like Peter, say it in my accent. If I'm on the block with the pimps and hustlers, break it down to me in jive talk, daddy. And if I'm a teen-ager, hip me to it in the latest words, 'cause we change some of our words very week.*

But above *all, put your money where your mouth is, as we gamblers say. "If he is the boss, the Lord, the Christ, tell us plainly by the way he rules your life." The world is listening to the speech made by our every action. You can't run around talkin' 'bout "He is the Christ" when you are plainly servin' somebody else everytime you speak to your own wife or husband. You can't call him Lord, Lord, and do not the things that he says on the job or in the school or in the city government. If he's Lord of Lords, you got to get together and help his will be done in city hall, and in the police department.*

14. It is in order that the church repent, but only up to a point. For there is an important sense in which the world's craving for clarity is a craving that we *should not* and *cannot* satisfy. Should not, because the kind of clarity that Mr. Average Man is seeking is what might

be described as computer clarity. There is grim point to that computer joke in which a man stands before this massive machine and asks, "Is there a God?" The answer comes back: "There is now."

15. Computers are eminently helpful with questions of fact and quantity, but what about questions that partake of mystery because they deal with loyalties and relationships? The church is always tempted to give easy answers to hard questions, to succumb to the heresy of exactness. There are questions of the heart that cannot be answered with the plainness of a TV commercial. The Bible is not an almanac nor the minister the answer.

14–15. *The world says, "If he is the Christ, tell us plainly in our own language and in a way that we can see." But that still won't guarantee they'll understand who he is. Jesus said you can't understand if you don't want to. So we must be sorry we haven't told it plain, but only so sorry. We can't make people understand, and that's a good thing. Some people want to do us like they do a computer: push our button and get an easy answer all typed out. Machines can talk about facts and measurements, but they don't know anything about the soul. You can't measure one, and you can't program it for the computer.*

16. My friend over at the university was right when he said that there are certain parts of life to which a man must respond as a poet. There is a dimension of depth and mystery to life that we dare not compromise. What is a tear, for example? Here it is right from the latest unabridged dictionary: "A tear is a drop of the

saline watery fluid continually secreted by the lacrimal gland between the surface of the eye and the eyelid, serving to moisten and lubricate these parts and keep them clear of foreign particles." This is a tear?

17. A while ago the pages of the *Saturday Review* carried a question from a disturbed mother who wanted to know what she should say to her preschool daughter who asked, "Where was I when you were a little girl?" Two answers came in. One woman said, "I had a four-year-old boy who asked me that and I told him the truth. Half of you was a little tiny egg without a shell waiting in a very special place inside my body all the time Mommy was a little girl. Then, when I became a lady, God helped Mommy's body to make a soft, warm place for you to grow, and your father planted a little seed that made your egg whole, and you grew." The other answer was sent in by a teaching nun in Missouri. "Where was I when you were a girl?" The answer is simple: "In the mind of God." Both answers have their place. But I suggest that the second is truer to life because it guards the mystery. The first is so factual that it obscures a deeper truth.

16–17. Some questions can't be answered by the scientist; they have to be answered by the poet. It may be the same man, but he has to answer it in a different way, from a different part of himself. You ask him, "What is a tear?" And the scientist in him says it's a saline, watery fluid from the lacrimal gland. But that ain't the half! *There's another side to a tear, a mystery that only his soul can look at. There is a measurement —a deepness, a quality to life that only the soul can begin to fathom. And when the world asks with its mind and measures, "Is this Christ?" it receives automatically an answer that fits: "Jesus was a human being. His fluids flowed when somebody made an incision in his side, etc." But when they ask from the soul, it's an altogether different proposition. Then you call on your own soul. Deep answers unto deep. The panorama of his person, the power of his command, the peculiar presence that is missed by man's measures—all these a soul can sense and try to translate. Sure, he had hands and feet. He ate and drank. He talked and walked— and prayed and cried. Any child can observe this. But my soul says he stood people on their feet. I have a professor in here [left chest] who starts a new kind of lecture when I read the Bible. And the most important things about Jesus begin to come into plain sight.*

18. Moreover, we *cannot* because the gospel to which we are committed is itself a mix of light and mystery. It is true that Saint Paul understands the gospel as the unveiling of a mystery. He writes to the Ephesians, "For he has made known to us in all wisdom and insight the mystery of his will, according to his purpose which he set forth in Christ . . ." (Ephesians 1:9). But this same apostle acknowledges in another place that we see as through a glass darkly and know only in part. Hugh Thompson Kerr in his very helpful book, *Mystery and Meaning in the Christian Faith*, points out that at every stage of Christian experience there is both meaning and mystery. It is not the case that, if I study hard enough and discipline myself sufficiently, light will break and all mystery disappear. No,

at every level of Christian experience there is both meaning and mystery.

18. *Unless you have that professor, all this will seem, at best, most mysterious. At worst, you'll think we're all a little off. And even with that inside teacher, we aren't expert on God. He's too big for that! Paul said, "Now we see through a glass darkly." We see and we get great help, but it's still misty. It's not clear yet. We can study and learn some things, even about God. But the dark glass won't be cleared away until later. Paul said, "Later, I'll know Jesus like he knows me already."*

19. Historically, the Roman Catholic Church has tended to perpetuate the mystery and Protestants have tended to emphasize meaning. This is why we are so word oriented in our Protestant tradition. We set out to explain it all. Isn't this basically what the word "obscene" means, to unbare that which rightly should be hidden. In our zeal to declare the truth we must remember that words alone cannot do it all because words tend to dissipate the very mystery in which we must participate.

20. Verbal exactness can be misleading. This is why we need to enlist the help of the poet, the dramatist, the artist, the musician, the dancer when we desire to communicate. A while ago Robert Frost's brief poem, "Stopping by Woods on a Snowy Evening" was analyzed by John Ciardi for two and a half long pages. People began writing in to ask that certain of Frost's images be defined. Frost, however, refused to be pinned down. He wished his readers to grapple with mystery themselves. This is why Lesslie Newbigin re-

minds us that "To see the whole truth of the situation you must read the fiction of our time as well as the scientific and technical journals. You must attend the theatre as well as the seminar. You must consult with the psychiatrist as well as the cyberneticians. When you do this, it is clear that there is another side to the picture."

19–20. (no translation)

21. Take for one example the mystery of good and evil. G. K. Chesterton wisely noted that "The troublesome thing about life is not that it is rational or irrational but that it is almost rational." Berdyaev said, "I should say that the problem of evil is a scandal to all monistic philosophy and so it is also to the traditional doctrine of Divine Providence."

22. Job grappled with the problem of how God could be reconciled to evil in the world, but was never given an answer. He was simply taken to a place where the mystery no longer disturbed his faith. We Christians get into real trouble when we attempt to interpret somebody else's providence to him. We have a way of rushing in where angels fear to tread. We would do well to remember a line from the hymn just sung: "Blind unbelief is sure to err, and scan his work in vain; God is his own interpreter, and he will make it plain."

21–22. Now it's not always easy. You can't explain the way Jesus deals with you to anybody. People who have no Christian faith think it's scandalous how good folks suffer sometimes. And you got no answer, and I ain't neither. But the great scholars have no answer either. There is no system that can explain it. No doc-

trine *that will put your mind at ease, let alone answer
somebody with no faith.*

*Job struggled and struggled. And when the book was
ended, he still didn't know why he suffered. He argued
around, and God left the argument in the Bible because it was healthy. But he never got an answer. But
he got in touch with God, and the scandalous question
of suffering didn't* bother *him anymore. Oh, he got his
possessions back. He was rich again. But that wasn't his
answer. His answer was just in* hearing *from God! It's
better to have God* chastise *you than not to hear from
him at all.*

Just the voice *of God, the still, small, inner voice, lays
all the questions to rest. And you can make it without
an answer for your head, after you have tried, if you
have an answer for your* heart *and soul! And God does
answer believing souls. "Blind unbelief is sure to err,
and scan his work in vain; God is his own interpreter,
and* he *will make it plain."*

23. A friend of mine killed a German soldier head-on
in World War II. In some ways as he tells it, it was an
unnecessary killing, at least it was to him. The fact that
the victim was an exceedingly youthful man burdened
his conscience all the more. Presently he was given a
Silver Star for this "achievement." But the star hung
heavy on his uniform and he sought counsel of three
different chaplains. Admittedly distraught and beside
himself, he walked into the office of the first chaplain,
flung the star down on the desk and said, "Here, justify
this!" The chaplain's answer was simply "Render unto
Caesar the things that are Caesar's." My friend grabbed

the star and said, "To hell with Caesar!" He went into the quarters of the second chaplain and the answer there was "Onward, Christian Soldiers." He took the star and went off to the third who happened to be a Southern Baptist preacher. "Justify this." The chaplain broke down and cried. Then they wept together. Finally they prayed. The soldier's question called not for clarity but for empathy.

24. "If thou art the Christ, tell us plainly." "If He is the Christ, tell us plainly." We work to clarify our words and meaning but we let the mystery stand. President Pusey of Harvard has said, "It would seem to me that the finest fruit of serious learning should be the ability to speak the word 'God' without reserve or embarrassment, certainly without adolescent resentment; rather with some sense of communion, with reverence and with joy." Surely we can wish this for ourselves and others.

23–24. As I close I want to tell you about a hard place where he made it plain. A young American in World War II killed a fine young German in a head-on battle. He was awarded the Silver Star for his bravery and he was probably promoted fast after that. But the face of a clean-cut youth dying at his hand haunted him. The medal hung heavy on his chest. It bothered him so bad that he had killed when he might have wounded that he couldn't sleep. The blood on his hands drove him through the door of three different chaplains. He demanded that each of them make it plain. He had to know if Christ could still be his Christ.

The first chaplain thought words would do it, and he quoted gravely, "Render unto Caesar the things that are Caesar's." The young man snatched the Silver Star off the chaplain's desk and stormed out of the chaplain's office, saying, "To hell with Caesar!" He went to a second chaplain, and this dear brother quoted "Onward, Christian Soldiers." Almost in rage, he dashed from the feeble presence of this sorry "sky pilot" and roared into the office of a down-home Baptist chaplain. At his wits' end, he demanded, "Justify this," as he threw the medal of courage on the third desk. The chaplain looked at the medal and looked at the man. He scanned his textbooks in his mind's eye, and he searched the scriptures frantically. But there was no plain word, and he finally looked back at the man and broke down crying. The young soldier couldn't stand it, and he wept too. When they had cried out their perplexity, the chaplain led in prayer. It wasn't very long. And it had no preaching parts. But when the prayer was over, the soldier looked out of wet eyes, and clasped the chaplain's hand in his trembling hand, while he barely managed to squeeze the word "thanks" past the huge lump that welled up in his throat.

But his face showed a peace that no word could describe or explain. Down deep he had heard the voice of the Christ he sought. He didn't know what the voice said, but just hearing it made him know that it was all right between them.

I imagine that if he'd known this song of Lucy Campbell's, he would have said, "That's it!" She wrote, one day:

Something within me, that holdeth the reign.
Something within me, that banisheth pain.
Something within me, I cannot explain.
All that I know, there is something within.

Related Reading

BLACK PREACHING: BOOKS

Pipes, William H. *Say Amen, Brother!* 1951. Reprint. Westport, Conn.: Negro Universities Press, 1970.

Rosenberg, Bruce A. *The Art of the American Folk Preacher*. New York: Oxford University Press, 1970.

BLACK PREACHING: ARTICLES

Freeing the Spirit (the magazine of Black liturgy published by the National Office of Black Catholics), vol. 1, no. 4; vol. 2, no. 1. These issues contain articles on Black preaching by editor Clarence Joseph Rivers, Olin P. Moyd, and Henry H. Mitchell.

Mitchell, Henry H. "Black Preaching". *Review and Expositor*, vol. 70, no. 3 (Summer 1973).

Morris, Calvin. "Martin Luther King, Jr., Exemplary Preacher". *The Journal of the Interdenominational Theological Center*, vol. 4, no. 2 (Spring 1977).

Spillers, Hortense J. "Martin Luther King and the Style of the Black Sermon". *Black Scholar*, September 1971.

PREACHING: BOOKS BY BLACKS

Ellison, John Malcus. *They Who Preach*. Nashville: Broadman Press, 1956. Now available through the author at Virginia Union University.

Johnson, Joseph A., Jr. *Proclamation Theology*. Shreveport, La.: Fourth Episcopal District Press (109 Holcomb Drive, 71103), 1977. Also contains chapters on Black Preaching.

Massey, James Earl. *The Responsible Pulpit*. Anderson, Ind.: Warner Press, 1974.

Taylor, Gardner C. *How Shall They Preach?* Elgin, Ill.: Progresive Baptist Publishing House (850 N. Grove Ave., 60120), 1977.

THE BLACK PREACHER AND ORATOR: RECENT

Boulware, Marcus H. *The Oratory of Negro Leaders: 1900-1968*. Westport, Conn.: Negro Universities Press, 1969.

Hamilton, Charles V. *The Black Preacher in America*. New York: William Morrow & Co., 1972.

Hicks, H. Beecher, Jr. *Images of the Black Preacher*. Valley Forge, Pa.: Judson Press, 1977.

COLLECTIONS OF BLACK SERMONS

Johnson, Joseph A., Jr. *The Soul of the Black Preacher*. Philadelphia: Pilgrim Press, 1971.

Newbold, Robert T., Jr., Ed. *Black Preaching: Select Sermons in the Presbyterian Tradition*. Philadelphia: The Geneva Press, 1977.

Payne, Daniel A. *Sermons and Addresses 1853-1891*. New York: Arno Press, 1972.

Philpot, William M., Ed. *Best Black Sermons*. Valley Forge, Pa.: Judson Press, 1972.

Scott, Manuel L. *From a Black Brother*. Nashville: Broadman Press, 1971; *The Gospel for the Ghetto*. Nashville: Broadman Press, 1973.

Smith, J. Alfred, Sr., Ed. *Outstanding Black Sermons*. Valley Forge, Pa.: Judson Press, 1976.

Young, Henry J., Ed. *Preaching the Gospel*. Philadelphia: Fortress Press, 1976.

Index

251